Balancing

Esther Naylor

ACKNOWLEDGEMENTS

I'd like to thank Zvi [Heniek] Kowalski for shedding some light on my parents' life in Poland. To Michael Berman who remembered his hunger on the ship *El Sedan* at the age of two and a half. To Mish Blacher [Becker], who was witness to the fiery discussions during some of the Jewish Progressive Centre meetings and anyone else who helped me along the way.

Thank you also to Michael, Anna and Kerry from Publish Central for the book cover and interior design.

To my parents
whose lives were valuable and valued.

First published in 2020 by Esther Naylor.
This edition published in 2023 by Esther Naylor.

© Esther Naylor 2023

The moral rights of the author have been asserted

All rights reserved. Except as permitted under the *Australian Copyright Act 1968* (for example, a fair dealing for the purposes of study, research, criticism or review), no part of this book may be reproduced, stored in a retrieval system, communicated or transmitted in any form or by any means without prior written permission.

All inquiries should be made to the author.

CONTENTS

Passover In Wloclawek Poland 1931	1
Passover 1931	5
The Celebration	8
The Kowadlo Family – Maneshtanah	10
Search For The Afakoiman	12
Concluding The Seder	13
Life	14
My Mother	16
Moshe Dancygier	32
Lights	42
Years Later	44
Wloclawek	49
September 24, 1939	52
Returning To Wloclawek For Eva	55
The Proposal	57
Resuming Their Lives	61
The Al Sudan	66
Australia	69
The Shopping Expedition	73
The Three Factories	76
The Second Factory	80
The Third Factory	84
Moving Forward	86
The Jewish Progressive Centre	91
Weekends	97
Christmas At The Beach	116
Passover In Australia	119
Cleaning	124
Queensland	127
Later Visits	132
Eva's Cousin Ange	134
Letterboxes	137
Making Latkes	140
Photos	143
Give Me Your Money	145

Melbourne	147
The Phone Call	149
The Apartment	151
The Hospital	153
Let's Go To America	155
The Getaway	158
A Meeting Is Held	160
Ambulance Needed	162
Get You Tonight	164
Death	170
The Move	172
My Daughter	174
Returning To Melbourne	178
The Funeral	180
Packing Up	182
Ripping Boxes	184
Afternoon At The Nursing Home	189
The Nursing Home	191
Around The Table With Eva	193
Where's Moshe	195
Returning That Night	202
I Said They Could Ring	204
The Following Day	206
Towards The End Of Her Life	207
Another Call	209
Wounded	212
Hospital	216
Caulfield Hospital Visiting Hours	219
The Man Beside Me	220
My Mother's Death	223
The Burial	230
Finality	232
Looking In	234
List Of Deceased Family Members	238
Glossary	242

PASSOVER IN WLOCLAWEK POLAND 1931
The Dancygier Family

In preparation for Passover a bunch of lively children, varying in age, candles and paper in hand, go silently from one kitchen cupboard to the next, meticulously collecting the tiniest remnant of Chametz: any product containing yeast.

The Chametz is taken to the kitchen table. It is tightly wrapped, ready for burning the following morning.

Dressed in traditional Hasidic garb; the boys are wearing small back skullcaps, their long side locks dangling. White open neck shirts and black straight-legged pants, tassels visible beneath their black vests.

The girls are dressed in ankle length skirts, blouses buttoned right to the neck and all the children are wearing closed lace up shoes.

Their mother is sitting at the table, overseeing their diligent efforts. She has on a long plain colourless dress and a grey headscarf tied in a knot behind her neck, accentuating her well-defined facial features.

In the yard, the following morning, warming themselves around the bonfire the children cheerfully toss their packages into the fire and watch the flames draw the Chametz to itself, like a creature with outstretched tentacles, enveloping and ingesting.

That night, filing into the well-used bathroom, each member of the Dancygier family jauntily step up to take their turn at the wash basin, customarily splashing their hands three times on one side and three on the other. Pouring water from the two-handled cup. Braine, the second oldest daughter, in dutiful assistance, provides them the ever-dampening towel.

In the impeccably clean dining room, nine members of the Dancygier family recline haphazardly to the left, around the large wooden table. Demeanours are relaxed, as on this festive night they are expected to be.

Moshe, aged thirteen, is a sensitive boy who does not disclose his feelings. He is mentally robust. His older sister, Braine, who is bossy, forced him to eat when he was a youngster. He is cheerful, talkative, and has short, thick, black, straight hair and prominent facial features. Brainer is striking, with brown curly hair and pale skin. Moshe's younger brother Hershl's facial features are similar to Moshe's, but he has brown, wavy hair. Toba, aged seven, is blonde. Her hair is slightly wavy and she has pale skin. Hena, is five years old with dark curly hair, darker skin and she is also talkative.

Their clothes are pristine.

The children's father, Sholem, is seated at the head of the table and his wife, Perl, a force to be reckoned with, is next to him. Perl's parents are also present.

Normally, there would be seven children at the Seder tonight, Fraidl, the oldest girl has joined her husband's family for Passover. Shlomo is also absent.

There is nothing extraordinary about the table setting except for the two ornate silver candle holders, probably passed down from the previous generation, and the perfectly pressed white table cloth.

Next to the ten white plates on the table, stand ten tiny dark green wine glasses, ready to be filled four times during the course of the night, ten Haggadahs, booklets, containing songs and texts which establish the order of proceedings at the Passover Seder, and a bottle of wine, placed in the centre of the table.

The Seder plate, containing Maror and Chezeres, Choroses, Ziroa and Karpas [bitter herbs, a mixture of nuts, raisins and wine, a roasted egg and bone vegetables such as potato, celery, parsley and horseradish] and the Matzos, have been placed closer to the head of the table; a small bowl of salted water beside them.

They sing a blessing over the Karpas [potato, parsley and celery] and in turn each person takes a tiny amount, dips it into the salted water and eats it.

PASSOVER 1931
The Kowadlo Family

In a neighbouring street in Wloclawek, the Kowadlo family, Eva, Ruth, Joseph, and Zygmus, their parents, Esther and Efroim and Efroim's parents, Eliezer and his wife Michla, are also celebrating Passover.

Eva is thirteen. She is reserved, intelligent, with an inner strength. She has below the ear light brown hair, classical looks and light blue eyes. Her sister Ruth, is eight, has brown eyes, is smart, inquisitive, with short dark hair, thick fringe and a lovely smile. Joseph is twelve, wiry, easy going, reflective and has light brown wavy hair. Zigmus, is five years old. He is adorable, playful, has a full face and light brown wavy hair. The boys are wearing skullcaps.

Their father, Efroim, makes shoes for a living. He plays cards in his spare time, is clean-shaven, wears a dark single-breasted suit with large rounded lapels, a white shirt, a thin dark knotted tie, a black skullcap and is bespectacled.

His wife Esther, a creative person, skilfully fashioned the chocolate and white striped sailor tops the children are wearing. She has a kind, oval shaped face with even features, has flawless skin, dark brown curly hair, is diminutive and well-proportioned. She is wearing a modest, tailored, woollen dress.

Eliezer is a Cantor, father of nine, a tough man who sent some of his children out to work at an early age. He has a long dark brown beard and is conservatively dressed; loose jacket, closed at the neck, and a raised felt skullcap and also wears spectacles.

His wife, Michla, is wearing a black dress, scooped at the neck, displaying a gold chain with an oval locket. She has sharp features and knowing eyes.

The women have uncovered, short, styled, brown hair.

Except for Eliezer, members of the family reflect, to a greater degree, fashionable attire in Poland in the 1930s.

The culinary aroma permeates the apartment and the ease at their dining table is palpable. They are all captivated and transported by Eliezer's resonant voice as he passionately sings the first prayer.

A white tablecloth also covers their simply set table. But in contrast to the Dancygier's Seder table, the white plates are rimmed with a colourful decorative floral motif and the candlestick holders adorning their table, while silver, are plain.

The tiny clear wine glasses sit upon tiny clear saucers. A bottle of red wine, the Seder plate and the three Matzos are also placed closer to the head of the table and everyone has a Haggadah next to their plate.

Ruth Kowadlo, Zygmus Kowadlo, Eva Kowadlo, Joseph Kowadlo

THE CELEBRATION
Dancygier

Sholem Dancygier takes the Matzos, which have been separated by a cloth and removes the middle one. He breaks it into two pieces and puts the smaller section back in between the other two. He wraps the larger one up for the Afakoiman a Matzo used in a game. It is to be hidden from the children.

He lifts the Afakoiman up onto his shoulders and says,
"In haste we left Egypt.
This is the bread of affliction, that our fathers ate in Egypt. Whoever is hungry let him come and eat.

Whoever is needy let him come and celebrate Passover. Now we are slaves, next year may we be free men."

Perl removes the Seder plate and they pour the second glass of wine for one another.

Sholem quickly scans the room.

"*Farmackhn deyne oign, kinderlech,*" he says.

"Close your eyes little children."

Toba tightly squeezes her eyes closed. Hena lowers her head and does likewise. Hershel and Braine cover their eyes with one hand. Moshe cups both hands over his face.... peeps through imperceptible spaces between his fingers, as does Hershl.

"Moshe, Hershl... close your eyes," Sholem says.

The boys take a quick look at each other and chuckle.

Sholem scans the room then hides the Afakoiman in the bookcase. He quickly turns back around, to ensure that nobody is peeping.

THE KOWADLO FAMILY – MANESHTANAH
The Four Questions

As a part of the Passover celebration the youngest boy is required to answer four questions; the same question is repeated four times.

Eliezer asks Zygmus, "Why is tonight different to all other nights?"

"On all other nights we eat Chametz and Matzos but tonight, only Matzos."

Second answer. "On all other nights we eat many vegetables but, on this night, we eat Maror."

Third answer. "On all other nights we do not dip even once but on this night, twice."

The last answer. "On all other nights we eat either sitting or reclining but on this night we all recline."

Zygmus begins singing the Maneshtanah. The others join in.

SEARCH FOR THE AFAKOIMAN

Dancygiers

The hunt for the Afakoiman begins. The children search every corner of the room, under chairs, table, cushions, behind members of the family and finally the in bookcase.

When Hena locates the Afakoiman, she triumphantly holds it up in the air.

"*Ich hab es gefunen. Ich hab es gefunen.*"

"I found it. I found it."

Toba chimes in, "*Ich hab es auch gefunen.*"

"I also found it!"

They are awarded one coin each.

CONCLUDING THE SEDER

Both families conclude their Seder by eating a small piece of Matzos before drinking the fourth glass of wine. Raising their glasses, they make a toast,

"Next year in Israel."

LIFE

My parents were both born in Wloclawek, a small town in Poland, one hundred and fourteen kilometres from Plock and one hundred kilometres from Warsaw. My mother was born in 1920 and my father in 1921.

I never met any of my father's family and he barely spoke about them but I do know it was a huge family, much bigger than my mother's.

Neither of my parents spoke much about their lives before or during the war. It came out in dribs and drabs. They preferred to concentrate on their new lives in Australia, a country they loved. They had arrived in

1948, with a baby, a very young child, a small brown suit case and five pounds, sent to them by an uncle and aunt who were their sponsors.

MY MOTHER
Eva

My mother Eva, was born into a traditional Jewish family which originally came from Lithuania. She was the oldest of four children.

Her home, in Ulicia Cygunka, incredibly, still exists today. It is a large flat roofed, now cracked and peeling, grey concrete apartment block, three and four storeys high and retains its white double-framed panelled windows looking out onto the narrow street.

Even in its existing state, I feel a sense of romance about the place. I imagine it in the pre-war years, bustling, with my mother, as a girl standing in front of the double glass doors, on the wrought iron enclosed balcony, talking to someone down below.

I can see her jumping rope in the street, with two of her best friends holding the rope at either end as she counts her skips, always trying for a higher number.

I imagine Joseph and Moshe, bouncing a ball. Joseph suddenly dropping the ball and jumping into the rope, teasing "You're going to fall. You're going to fall." Eva pushing him out. Moshe leaping in and comically, hopping on alternate legs, his eyes fixed upon Eva.

The plot of grass opposite the building with three remaining trees might have been part of the communal garden where families once gathered and children played, although, the apartment block did include a communal courtyard.

Wloclawek was a vital town with a very strong community spirit, home to 13,500 Jewish people, many of them Hasidim.

Eva Kowadlo (right) with friend. Poland

Michla Kowadlo

Eliezer Kowadlo

Esther and Efroim Kowadlo

My father Moshe used to visit the Kowadlo family at Ulicia Cyganka, when he was a boy, with his long side locks and when he was older, with a wispy brown beard.

The Kowadlos were a large family with countless cousins, many uncles and aunties and two sets of grandparents. They were passionate about music and loved to sing. Eva's cousin, Heniek, who migrated to Israel from Poland after World War II, was a constant visitor and described Eva's home as a place where people were warmly received and visiting there, always a delight.

The love for singing and playing musical instruments flowed down into future generations. On a professional level, there is a Professor of Music, a concert Pianist and another Cantor.

Eva's paternal grandfather Eliezer was a Cantor, and a Mohel, a man who circumcises Jewish boys, eight days after their birth.

Eva's father Efroim liked to treat his children to chocolates, probably establishing the basis for Eva's lifetime affection for them.

Her mother Esther Kowalski, excelled in craft work and cookery. I inherited her name and size.

Eva joined the Communist party when she was a teenager, as did many people in Poland. The nineteens, twenties and thirties were economically difficult years in Wloclawek. Many people were forced to send their children to work in order to put food on the table.

My parents were very idealistic. They wanted to change the world, to help improve conditions for everyone. They believed in equality and that the Socialist and Communist Parties were the parties most likely achieve this. Prior to marrying my father, who she saw simply as a friend of her younger brother, Eva had been in love with an older boy, whose commitment to social justice was so great, that he joined a group in Poland, opposed to Fascism, and with them, set off to fight in the Spanish Civil War. Sadly, he never returned home.

There is a photo of my mother in a book written about Wloclawek titled,

FROM THE REVOLUTIONARY TRADITIONS OF WLOCLAWEK

kujawsko-pomorskie, cultural society, 1965

Her photo is in the chapter titled: "Akcje bezrobotnych," which means, "Shares of the unemployed."

At the time, Eva believed that the Communist Party best represented the values she held, but later, she became disillusioned with Communism and thought that those values had been lost, and replaced with cold, hard, dogma, having no regard for human rights and it was human rights that both my parents also strove for, while members of the Jewish Progressive Centre, in Australia.

My great grandparents, Eliezer and his wife Michla, had nine children.

One of the boys, a violin player, went to work at the age of twelve. Another followed in his father's footsteps, becoming a Cantor and Mohel [Circumciser]. He sang at the St. Kilda Synagogue in Melbourne, Australia. To my knowledge, six of the children survived the Second World War by leaving Poland, four migrated to Australia, the rest to America.

Efroim, the oldest child, stayed in Poland.

He perished along with Esther, Ruth, Zygmus, Eliezer and Michla.

They banged on the door with pistols in hand.

The old man opened it slowly but soon could not stand.

His wife heard the commotion and ran in to see.

They blew her away instantaneously.

My mother was a very attractive, shy and unassuming woman, although after my father's death she became much more assertive. She spoke Polish, Yiddish, English and Russian and could understand German, was a stickler for correct pronunciation and erupted into peals of laughter at some of my attempts to speak Polish.

She loved to read, listen to music and sing along but could not abide anyone singing out of tune. Even in some of her darkest moments at the nursing home, she was able to block out all thoughts and sounds, allowing the music to infuse her mind. She closed her eyes, creatively twirling her hands through the air, in time to it.

She was a charming person, an excellent hostess and cook who thoroughly enjoyed her food, especially desserts. Eating them very slowly, savouring every mouthful. Lightly gliding her folk or spoon down and around the outside of the sweet, evening it out, keeping it balanced until nothing was left.

She also had an acute wit but absolutely no idea of how marvellously funny she could be. My daughter and I laughed so hard at one of her comments that we missed our turn off, on the freeway.

It was my father who did most of the yelling and she allowed it, to a point. But she stood her ground when it was important to her. And sometimes when confronted with an argument, she replied with a humorous retort.

"Look! He thinks he's King Farouk."

When I was a teenager, I usually left getting out of bed for school, until the very last minute and so I asked my mother to determinedly wake me up earlier in the morning. Then, when she did, I yelled at her for continuously coming into my bedroom to wake me. Poor woman she could not win either way.

I dashed into the shower for a two-minute blast, brushed my teeth, dragged the hair brush with a few missing tufts, through my shoulder-length fair hair, threw on my school uniform; yellow shirt, grey tunic, grey blazer, brown stockings and brown school shoes. Grey felt beret in winter. Yellow checked dress and a light straw boater hat in summer. And flew out of the back door. Though, not before seizing a piece of rye bread and vegemite, waiting on a small white plate on our marbled, circular, Laminex kitchen table, prepared for me by my very patient mother. When there was more time it would be accompanied by a soft-boiled egg.

It was fortunate that my relationship with my mother was a good one. She never judged me and she trusted me completely. She barely exhibited any anger.

There were a couple of times when we had words but I recall nothing major. In those cases, her comments could be quite cutting.

She made it perfectly clear that she was not happy for me to marry a non-Jew. But when faced with my decision to do so, both of my parents were genuinely pleased for me and soon afterwards honestly loved my husband.

When I was about eight I remember, she chased me around the dining room table, trying to catch me, to give me a smack for something or other I had done.

It was the next year, when I was swinging on the monkey bar at the local park with a couple of my friends and accidentally cracked my head. It bled quite a lot, so my friends took me home.

I was sitting on a high wooden bench in the bathroom while my mother washed my wound, when my friends returned to ask if they could borrow my skipping rope which, I had promised to lend it to them prior to the accident. My mother was furious. Also, once, after a visit to our family dentist in North Carlton, who had unsuccessfully attempted to get me to keep my mouth open so that she could insert the drill, eventually giving up, and suggesting that we go to the Dental Hospital instead, a bit of anger was exhibited as we walked home down the cobbled lane way next to the surgery,

On another occasion, we were standing in a long queue at a local picture theatre. I was twelve years old. I suddenly broke into Yiddish. She looked astounded, answering me in English, which was unusual. When we got home she said to my father, "She doesn't want to speak one word of Yiddish and there, in the foyer, she suddenly launches into the language."

Tim Naylor, Esther Naylor

Balancing

Tim Naylor, Eva Berman

Once, as a teenager, I used some undesirable language, which hurt her and she began to cry. She was insulted and thought it unjustified. I can understand why it affected her that way now, having felt the same when my own children have spoken harshly to me.

At the nursing home, in the latter stages of her life however, she was the one who shocked everyone with language that I had never heard her use.

Furthermore, she did not appreciate being patronised and made it quietly, but pointedly clear to anyone who may have talked to her as though her level of intelligence had entirely diminished.

In 2011, I received a very moving email from Zach, a thirteen-year-old boy, from America, who was about to be Bar Mitzvoth.

In Burke Virginia, where he attended school, the students were given an assignment. They were to look through the Yad Veshem website and find the names of young Jewish boys who perished during World War II, before the age of thirteen, to honour, as a ceremonial twin, during their own Bar Mitzvah.

Zach found Zygmus Kowadlo.

In his own words Zach said:

"I am honoured to be able to do this for Zygmus and for your family and I hope to hear back from you and I am sorry for your loss. Zygmus will always be remembered."

He asked me if I would write a letter as if I were Zygmus, so that he could read it out during his ceremony. I was very moved and agreed to do it.

Zach made a plaque and a tallis, a prayer shawl, in Zygmus's honour and would wear the tallis when he read from an old Torah, which had been rescued from Poland, after the war.

Dear Zach

I am writing to congratulate you on the occasion of your Bar Mitzvah.

I'm so happy that you chose me as your ceremonial twin. I can see that you are a person who really cares about others by the time and trouble you took in making the tallis, prayer shawl, and plaque for me.

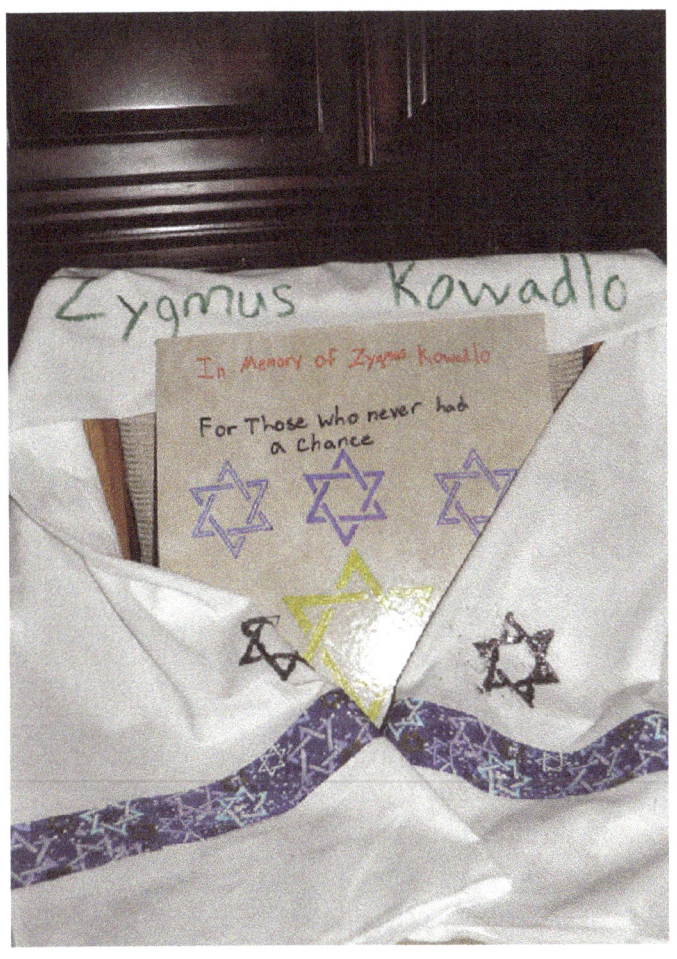

Plaque and prayer shawl

As you know, I come from Wloclawek in Poland. I was the youngest of four children. Eva was the oldest, eight years older than me. Then Joseph, Ruth and me. I was the baby. I was very much loved by my siblings, especially by Eva who thought I was the sweetest thing she had ever seen.

My parents did not feel they could leave Wloclawek during the war because of their own parents and their two young children. They could never have imagined what was to come. But Eva and her brother Joseph together with Moshe Dancygier who later became Moshe Berman and married Eva were lucky enough to flee Poland and finally make it to Australia.

Even though we come from different times and countries we still have things in common. We're both kids who enjoy playing games and we are both Jewish boys with loving families.

My grandfather and uncle were both Cantors and in our family we all love to sing. So, let's celebrate at your Bar Mitzvah. Let's dance and have some fun and of course hope that there are a few good presents in there too.

I truly wish you all the best.
And Zach thanks for acknowledging my life.
Yours sincerely
Zygmus Kowadlo

Zach's father Alan wrote:

"I can't tell you how much this means to us to be able to communicate and do this in honour for Zygmus and your family. He is now inexorably tied to Zach's Bar Mitzvah. May his memory always be a blessing. We hope this offers your family some peace and comfort to know that Zygmus will never be forgotten."

It is amazing to think that somewhere across the other side of the world, someone had found my mother's young brother on a website and had given him a Bar Mitzvah.

MOSHE DANCYGIER

My father, came from an Ultra-Orthodox Jewish family, Ger. Hasidim, which originated in Gora Kalwaria a small town in Poland. The third youngest of seven children, he became interested in Socialism in his early teens. He began to question his faith and wondered how he could leave the fold.

He decided to go to a Socialist Party meeting in the town, without the knowledge of either of his parents. Shocked, upon discovering his whereabouts, his father Sholem dashed to the meeting, found Moshe and dragged him out by the ear.

"*Zey nisht aza lobus aun geyn der rekhte veg.*"

"Don't waste your time and follow the right path."

His mother Perl Bergman, born in Konstantin, was one who demanded supreme perfection.

Once, when my father was a young boy, she asked some of her children to keep an eye on the bread she was baking; to turn the oven off at the appropriate time so that she could go to the market square, with my father. It was a place where shoppers thronged, bargaining, or met with friends. She had an independent stall there. Her stall was one of many. It was small and tent like, had a flat canvas roof and was surrounded by stone, spired, bi-coloured two and three-storey, chimneyed buildings.

When they returned, she opened the front door and while still only at the bottom of the staircase, she tilted her head upward slightly, inhaled and was accosted, she said, by the smell of burning bread. She cried,

"Auy! Dos broyt is shoyn farbrent!"

"Oh, the bread is already burnt!"

The oldest child Fraidl, was married to David Goldberg when war broke out.

Moshe's older brother, Shlomo, a merchant, was also married. He and his wife, had moved to Lodz, so that he could undertake Rabbinical studies. My father thought there was a possibility, that either he or his wife and child may have escaped to America. This could never be confirmed.

Balancing

Moshe Dancygier (Berman)

Moshe Berman

I don't know much about his three sisters, Braine, Toba and Hena, except that Braine, who was older than my father, was quite bossy.

My father recalled that one of his sisters was extremely beautiful and was noticed by a talent scout when the family, were promenading along busy Piekarska Street, home to many Hasidim, with its old stone, double and triple storey buildings and quaint glass front shops, where people occasionally stopped to chat, or gathered on street benches.

The scout followed them home and asked Sholem if he would allow his daughter to compete in a beauty contest which was to be held in one of the larger towns in Poland. Sholem would not give his permission.

I know that my father was very fond of Harshl, his younger brother. He said he would have supported him in any way he could. Before the war, Harshl worked as a shop assistant.

Although I always knew that my father would do anything for me or any member of our family, my relationship with him was fraught with conflict.

As a child, I thought he was quite frightening and overbearing at times, with his shocking temper and acerbic tongue and he always had to know our whereabouts.

Sometimes when I was somewhere I was probably not meant to be, I felt like he was driving past looking for me. It was unnerving.

He did not take kindly to impertinence.

"*Farmachn dos mol, di herst. Eider ich geb dir a flusk!*" "You'd better shut your mouth, do you hear, before I give you a smack!"

Or sometimes "*Du makhts dos oif zelachohas?*" "Are you doing that out of spite?"

And saying "Shut Up" was for him a criminal offence for which there was no punishment harsh enough.

My powers of discernment, in regards to when I had said enough, had not yet been developed.

However, there were never any restrictions upon me as a teenager, when it came to my social life, except when I went out with boys, there was one rule I had to abide by no matter what: that I arrive home by midnight. If for any reason I was late, he would be pacing up and down the street in his pyjamas, waiting for me and it was certain there was trouble ahead.

His habit of waiting for our safe return never abated but grew to include my children.

My father was about five foot nine inches tall, body spry. He had thick black hair, dark skin in summer, brown eyes and a Roman nose. He was an outgoing person, with a remarkable zest for life and one who liked to organise his days.

His creativity and determination were never in question. He could make or fix anything and his generosity was overwhelming; continuously giving to various charitable organisations and to us.

Whether he was entertaining or simply lending a hand, nothing was too much trouble for him. Anyone who came to our house for dinner or celebrations was made to feel especially welcome.

Once after transitioning from the clothing manufacturing business into the building industry, he installed a new kitchen for an aunt and uncle. He arrived at their house on the weekend and worked for hours until the kitchen was completed, refusing any payment whatsoever.

He also renovated a bathroom for me, which ended up being the nicest room in our old Edwardian house.

And on occasions he scrubbed my saucepans until they sparkled. He altered my clothes when I needed them done and usually drove me or picked me up from any location I happened to be in, when I asked him to.

He usually stood up for his beliefs. Once, when he was walking through Surfers Paradise, he noticed a book written by a well-known Holocaust denier, displayed in the front window of the book store. Enraged, he went into the store and demanded that the they remove the book immediately, telling them that he had lived through the Holocaust in Europe and assured them, that it did happen. The sales assistant, removed the book from view. He passed the bookshop many times after that incident. The book was no longer in view.

On another occasion my parents were driving along Hoddle Street, Collingwood, and he suddenly pointed to the motorbike in front of him and exclaimed, "Look, the man on the bike. He's got a swastika on his jacket!"

"Stop it Moshe. Don't get so agitated," Eva said.

"You cannot drive around with a swastika. He must be a Nazi."

They pulled up at the lights and Moshe unlocked his car door.

"No Moshe. Don't confront him."

But he jumped out of the car and approached the motorbike rider.

"Take your jacket off!" he yelled at him.

"What?" the rider asks, incredulous.

"Take that jacket off. You are wearing a Nazi swastika. Millions of people were murdered under that sign. Take it off or I'll smash into your bike."

The motorbike rider stared at Moshe, then, he removed his jacket, saying, "You are mad."

Moshe got back into the car.

Eva said, "Moshe, what's the matter with you?" "*Bist du faruked tze vus?*" "Are you crazy or what? You have to think before you do something like that. Do you know him? Do you know how he'll react?"

He definitely believed in the traditional roles for men and women, that is to say, until Eva's cooking skills began to diminish. Except for some weekends, when he liked to make onion omelettes, after which, we were coaxed, no, dragged, outside into the garden and allocated a section of it to weed.

"No, I don't want to weed under the rose bushes.

Look it's perfect. It doesn't need weeding." My protests were always in vain.

He took over the cooking quite easily and began taking an interest in cooking shows. He looked up old recipes that luckily had been scribbled down, such as, my Russian aunt's six egg sponge cake, which always rose to a mighty height and various stews which he mastered and enjoyed eating; one of them becoming his signature dish.

He said he learnt to cook from "The Big One" on television, which is how he referred to Ian Hewison, a chef on a television cooking show. But the chicken soup and the latkes, were Eva's dishes. Cooking those dishes was ingrained.

Moshe Berman

LIGHTS

My father was also the one who came into my room to see what the matter was when I was scared and called out for my mother in the middle of the night.

I was about four years old and saw a large configuration of floating lights on my bedroom ceiling.

I watched them, fascinated, for some time, but after a while I wanted them to go. I opened and closed my eyes a number of times but they remained. I became frightened and yelled,

"MUM!"

No answer.

"Mum, Mum," I cried.

My parents were sound sleepers.

After a few more calls my father came into the room.

"What's the matter?"

"I want Mum."

"She's asleep. What is it?"

"There are lights moving around the ceiling! They won't go away."

He turned on the light 'Look there's nothing there," he assured me.

We said goodnight but once my father had left the room the pattern of lights reappeared.

I wanted them gone.

"MUM!"

My father came back into my room. "Leave the light on," I said, "They won't go."

And so, he did.

YEARS LATER

Years later my mother used to say, "You're just like your father."

And that would have been the greatest insult to me. But I'd probably picked up his facade of toughness because that's what we often do as children; pick up the characteristics of those we consider to be stronger than ourselves.

And I'd spent years toughening up to survive what I thought was his tyrannical reign.

And when I was older I spent quite some time getting back at him, wasted time behaving hurtfully.

But it's hard to recover those memories now and really, they are not important to me anymore because I found that when you forgive someone something, whatever is forgiven, seems to fade from your consciousness and I forgave him years ago, long before I began to understand why he acted the way he did. And I hope he forgave me too.

Of course, he mellowed greatly over the years.

And I realised that he was not that tough at all. He simply kept his emotions close to his chest and they often poured out as anger. He too was trying to survive.

I had to take in and it took me some time, that he had come from an Ultra-Orthodox upbringing and way of life, which was so strict, regimented and all encompassing. And that at eighteen, like many other young Jews who came from Nazi occupied Europe he was forced into a labour camp where he was brutalised. That he fled his homeland at nineteen, constantly eluding German patrols, taking refuge in Russia where life was also difficult. His entire family had been annihilated. He travelled across the world for a renewed life: a different sense of being, with a new language, a different culture and a new way of thinking and behaving. And that what I had experienced as controlling behaviour was for him, not only his authoritarian outlook, but also a way of keeping what he had, his family, close to him.

I was astounded when I discovered that he was an Ultra-Orthodox Jew right up until the Second World War and I wondered how much of it had actually stayed with him.

He wore a hat, a dark grey soft wool fedora, well into the 1950s. I was always under the impression he wore that hat because it was the fashion for men at the time but now remembering conversations between my father and an uncle and considering his upbringing, I have concluded that it was actually because he felt more comfortable with his head covered.

"I see you're not wearing your hat anymore, Moshe," a comment made by my uncle, as we all walked down a busy inner-city road where, due to his Mediterranean appearance, he was once more approached by a person speaking to him in Italian.

"No, I don't need it anymore," he replied.
"It's not fashionable to wear hats anymore."
"But you don't wear it for that reason."

Eva and Moshe Berman

"Yes – but I don't need it anymore."

On our last Jewish New Year celebration together, the year before he died, when the table was set and we were all about to sit down for dinner, he left the lounge-room, reappearing a couple of minutes later, wearing his Tallis and skull cap and without any pomp or formality proceeded to cut the Challah.

I don't think he would have considered being religious again but he did miss the company of Jewish people, when my parents moved to Queensland and so he visited the synagogue, to make some Jewish acquaintances.

In the end he was definitely evaluating his life but what his conclusions were, nobody will ever know.

WLOCLAWEK

The Germans marched into Wloclawek in September 1939 and with the assistance of many Poles, immediately set about the eradication of the Jewish community, which consisted of approximately 13,500 Jews out of a population of 60,000.

It was the first town in Poland to enforce the wearing of a gold patch.

Synagogues were burnt down, Jewish leaders shot, Jewish property looted and eight hundred residents, including Moshe, were rounded up. People began moving to other towns. Those more fortunate left the country.

In November 1940, the remaining 3000 Jews were forced into a Ghetto and in December the ghetto was sealed off; food became scarce, people starved and contracted various diseases.

Even with conditions as hideous as this, Jewish cultural life was still maintained. People met secretly at the Jewish cemetery. It also served as a book exchange and a place for theatrical performances, right up until late 1942. It was then, that the last of the surviving Jews in Wloclawek were sent to Chelmno, extermination camp where they were gassed.

Initially there's blame for all of your woes, then you isolate, degrade and dehumanise. Because how could anyone ever do that to a person, a human being?

You would never do that to my child, my parents, my grandparents, my friends or even to me?

Remove, rape, maim, gas, burn and kill. Finally, you found your solution.

Most of my mother's family and as far as I know, all of my father's family were taken to Chelmno extermination camp, in the Polish village of Chelmno nad Nerem and gassed.

They were transported by train to a nearby railway station; put into closed cattle wagons or sometimes made to walk in freezing conditions, tormented and brutalised along the way.

320,000 people were murdered in the two sites used for exterminating. One was The Palace, a large manor house also serving as the reception centre.

People were tricked into thinking there was work for them on the estate but they soon discovered they were trapped behind barred doors. Horrific screams, hysteria, cries to God but eventually there was silence.

Shovel them in. Shovel them in.

The other site was the Rzuchen forest, two and a half kilometres away where slaughtered Jewish bodies were buried in mass graves, like rubbish at the local tip, carelessly shovelled into a heap, one on top of the other, piled on, shovelled in.

SEPTEMBER 24, 1939

At the age of eighteen, Moshe and eight hundred others from Wloclawek were taken to prison, systematically beaten and tortured. Soon after their arrival, a number of young people, who appeared to be in good health, were selected and transferred to slave labour camps where, throughout the day, they were subjected to further horrific treatment.

It was when the selected group lined up to be registered, asked to give their full names, that my father decided not to give his family name, Dancygier, instead, giving his mother's less Jewish sounding name, Bergman. The officer writing down the details left the letter "g" out of Bergman and my father did not correct him. And so, our name became Berman.

For the sake of amusement, German guards placed Moshe up against a wall with his hands raised above his head, vociferously, deciding at which point to pull the trigger; pretending to shoot. And at the very last moment changing their minds. Devastatingly perverse mind games were just a bit of fun for the day.

A Nazi officer forced Moshe to expose his genitals and was about to cut off his penis when he was interrupted by other officers entering the room. The Nazi quickly put his knife back into his pocket and ordered Moshe, "OUT!"

Sometime later, he was shoved into an office, wrongfully accused of stealing. He was beaten ruthlessly and hit over the back of the head and neck with a rifle.

The Nazi saw a sharpened pencil on his desk. He grabbed it and dug it into Moshe's ear. Injuries which affected him for the rest of his life.

In the midst of the onslaught, a disturbance was heard outside in the yard.

An officer called out from the next room. Moshe's abuser left to investigate. In a split second, knowing that he was going to be killed, and with his characteristic ingenuity, he jumped out of the window and hid until he thought it was safe to leave. His exact circumstances are unclear. The most important thing is, that he was able to escape and survive.

RETURNING TO WLOCLAWEK FOR EVA

Leaving their large families behind in Wloclawek, carrying very few possessions, hiding by day and travelling at night, enduring all kinds of weather conditions, Eva and Moshe set out on a three-month walk navigating their way through the heavily wooded Białowieża forest, constantly avoiding German patrols in order to get to the Russian border.

On one occasion, a farmer who, prior to the war, had sold produce to Moshe's mother Perl for her market stall, hid them in his barn. He instructed them to remain hidden at all times, as he could neither vouch for the trustworthiness of his own wife nor, for his three daughters.

He also informed them that the Germans came to the farm every day between six and seven o'clock in the morning to check for strangers.

The Nazis arrived. Moshe and Eva were hiding in a crate of hay. The Nazis began viciously stabbing the hay with their bayonets, missing the sides of their heads and bodies by only a slight margin.

Other farmers however were not as compassionate as my grandmother's supplier. They ordered their dogs to attack them and yelled, threateningly.

THE PROPOSAL

During their time in the Białowieża forest, Moshe, who was in love with Eva, decided to ask for her hand in marriage. Having no experience expressing his intimate feelings, he casually said, letting down his guard;

"*Vilstu husene habn Eva?*"

Eva, unaware that this was a proposal, replied,

"*Nisht punktlech itst. Neyn.*"

"*Neyn,*" he says "*Ich mein, mit mir?*"

Surprised she says,

"*Ich veys nisht. Ich hab nisht getrucht vegn dem.*"

"Trakht vegn dem Eva. Ich sog dir tsu, aoyb di vest husene hobn mit mir, veln mir voynen in a shayn hoyz mit tzvai shlof tzimer un a shaynm Kuch," he says.

She laughs.

"Azoy? Dos volt gevein zaer gut. Ich val fun dem itst truchtn."

"Do you want to get married, Eva?"

Unaware that this was a proposal, Eva replied,

"Not precisely now, no."

"No, I mean, with me," he says.

Surprised she says, "I don't know, I've never thought about it."

"Think about it, Eva. I promise you that if you marry me, we'll live in a lovely house with two bedrooms and a beautiful kitchen."

She laughs.

"Really! Two bedrooms. And, a beautiful kitchen! That sounds very good. I will think about it."

Out of nowhere, two German officers and a Wehrmacht soldier appear. "HALT!" Chilled, their laughter ceases. They are instantly searched, money taken. *"ErschiesB sie!"* one of the Officers orders the Wehrmacht soldier. "Shoot them."

He marched my parents deeper into the woods, well out of sight. He turned, raised his gun and fired two bullets into the air.

"I am not going to shoot you," he said compassionately. "I have children the same age as you, at home."

He pointed and said, "Go that way and you'll be able to cross the border safely without running into any German patrols."

When Eva and Moshe finally caught sight of the border, they charged frantically towards it, hearts thumping, running towards what they believed was freedom. At the barricade they were mistaken for German spies and taken by lorry, to Magnitogorsk, a camp, in the Ural Mountains.

It was the end of March 1941.

They stayed in the camp for a number of years, working and learning the Russian language. It is possible that father worked in a granary and also had some involvement with the Soviet Partisan Army.

My mother spoke Russian well and did so on occasion, right up until three days before her death.

In 1945, when Moshe and Eva returned to Wloclawek to look for any surviving family members, Moshe was assured by a family friend that his entire family had been rounded up and taken to Chelmno.

"*Moshe du host kainem nicht tsu zuchn. Zey zanen ale toit.*" "Moshe, you've got no one to look for. They are all dead."

RESUMING THEIR LIVES

At the conclusion of World War II, amidst great confusion, millions of displaced people endeavoured to resume their lives but most of them had no home to return to and no desire to go back to their countries of origin, except of course, to look for any surviving relatives or friends.

To help them transition, DP [Displaced Persons] camps were created in Germany, Austria and Italy.

At the end of 1946 it was estimated that there were 250,000 DPs and that 185,000 were in Germany. Allied authorities and the United Nations Relief Rehabilitation Administration, UNRRA administered the camps.

The UNRRA established a Central Tracing Bureau so that DPs could find missing relatives and friends who had survived the War. Public radio broadcasts and newspapers were also used for this purpose.

The camps were sometimes airports, converted hospitals and summer camps for children, German army barracks and even concentration camps.

Although poverty and starvation prevailed, basic food, clothing and some medical care was provided. People were registered and transportation to their new homeland was organised.

My parents were lucky enough to be in a DP camp in Ainring, Germany, because in 1947, all the camps were closed and people were left to survive without any assistance whatsoever.

Most refugees in Ainring were, like my parents, from Poland and had fled to Russia during the war. It was situated near the Austrian border and had once been an airfield.

Jewish life and culture, was not only reborn but thrived in the camps. Synagogues and Jewish schools were set up where Yiddish and Hebrew were spoken and teachers were recruited from various countries around the world. Orchestras and theatres were also established.

Acting group. Moshe Dancygier (Berman) second from right

Moshe Dancygier (Berman), Michael Berman

Moshe Dancygier (Berman), Michael Berman, Eva Berman (Kowadlo)

Moshe Dancygier (Berman), Esther Berman, Eva Berman (Kowadlo)

Moshe performed in a variety of Yiddish plays. I saw a photo of him when he was an actor there, with his beard, but I assumed it was a false one, simply put on for the occasion.

Most people in the DP camps chose to go to Palestine, now Israel, but many also went to the United States of America and to a lesser extent, Australia, who in 1947 accepted 182,159 refugees.

Eva had relatives in Australia who were eager to sponsor our family, so instead of their initial choice, the United States, my parents decided on Australia.

We set sail from Marseilles, France on 26 of January 1948, on the Al Sudan. The journey probably took around six weeks.

THE AL SUDAN

The Al Sudan was a large Egyptian steamship used by the International Refugee Organization to bring about 164,100 displaced people from Germany to Australia, via Marseilles, France.

It was originally built as a cargo vessel to accommodate 770 people but it carried well over one thousand to Melbourne in 1948, using the cargo hold as additional accommodation.

Relatives already living in Australia sponsored most of the DPs. Jewish organisations and other altruistic people were also sponsoring. My husband's father, a Christian, was one of them. It was the sponsor's responsibility to organise accommodation and employment for the displaced people.

The meals on board the ship, were very basic. My brother, who was just over two years old at the time, remembers being constantly hungry and eating soap, which he thought, was cheese. Seasickness was also a problem for many people.

Men and women slept on bunks in separate areas. During the day the women helped in the kitchen while the men cleaned up on deck or in the engine room.

My parents were able to learn a few basic English words and sentences in the on-board English classes.

Children were bathed on deck in a small metal tub and when it was my turn, I was told that my loud screams could be heard all over the ship. My father said that at first people were confused and tried to locate the source of the cries but eventually they realised that it was me having a bath.

Emotions ran high as the ship approached the shore, with passengers thronging the decks for the best vantage point, eager for a glimpse of their new homeland.

BALANCING

Holding tightly to children, bundles and cases, hundreds of bodies, disparate, move in succession, over the gangway, spilling into Australia, the land of plenty.

AUSTRALIA
Land of Plenty

The green bus stops at the busy intersection. Moshe and Eva alight. They wait on the footpath for the lights to change from red to green.

A conversation ensues, in Yiddish.

"*Ich darf aribe geyn. Es is sheyn shpet.*"

Eva is concerned about arriving at work on time. She is on her way to the large fabric factory on the adjacent corner, where she works as a machinist.

The lights finally change.

A well-dressed man in his forties, standing next to them, overhears their conversation, eyes them both with suspicion and mutters "Speak English" as he quickly brushes past.

Eva ran across to the large grey brick building on the corner, leaving Moshe to wait for his tram.

He takes a tram into the city where he intends to evaluate men's trousers sold at a major city department store.

After arriving in Australia, he had worked for others, initially as a caretaker and then in a clothing factory. He decided, after much thought, that it was the right time and that he was prepared to take a risk, with his own business venture. After all wasn't this Australia, the land where opportunities abound? He was driven by the desire to create something of his own; a business he could develop and build upon, for himself and for his family and he concluded that manufacturing men's trousers would be a most prudent choice.

He enters Myer Melbourne and heads directly to the Men's section, where he carefully studies the selection of trousers on display. He considers their design and quality, running his thumb and fingers through the material.

He selected five pairs in his size, all varying in shades of brown and grey, and takes them into the fitting room to gauge their comfort and look.

Michael and Esther Berman

Happy with his decision he emerged carrying one dark grey pair, which he took to the counter. He paid for them and left the department store.

That night, at the conclusion of our meal, my father meticulously cleaned the kitchen table and unrolled the brown paper, bought specifically for the purpose of making a pattern. A pattern he continuously modified and perfected. He spread it out onto the table and laid the already unpicked trousers sections onto it, flattening them down and smoothing them out with the palms of his hands. With great care and precision, he began cutting out the patterns.

THE SHOPPING EXPEDITION

Eva's decision to begin migrant English classes was definitely hastened by the hostile reactions she received when she spoke Yiddish in the street.

Although her knowledge of English was limited, she had an excellent facility and enthusiasm for languages. However, she questioned her ability to ever master English, a language so very different to anything she had heard before, or had ever tried to pronounce.

A shopping expedition was organised to familiarise her with the names of various food items and to give her a little confidence when shopping independently. Eva was accompanied by her aunt, who spoke perfect

English, and was also her sponsor and by her two small children.

They stood at the counter of the local General Store, waiting for their turn to be served.

On the opposite side of the counter, the shop assistant carefully weighed a few slices of sausage meat on his scales, attempting to achieve the precise weight requested by the customer.

While adding a couple of extra slices, the customer raised his pointer finger into the air and exclaimed, "Dadledo!" The assistant wrapped up the meat, handed it to the customer and received his payment.

The procedure was repeated several more times; the customer saying, "Daddledo", after which the shop assistant wrapped the item.

When it was Eva's turn, she listened closely to the conversation between her aunt and the shop assistant, expecting the same sequence of events to transpire, but they did not.

Once outside the store, unable to contain her curiosity, she asked her aunt,

"*Vos is dos, Daddledo? Aleh zogn daddledo.*"
"What is this Daddledo? Everyone says Daddledo."
Her aunt laughed,

"*Es meynt, dos is genug. Ober du zog nisht azoy. Di darfs zogn.*"

"It means that is enough. But don't say it like that. They are pronouncing it incorrectly. You have to say. That will do or that is enough, thank you."

THE THREE FACTORIES

The first factory consisted of one room, downstairs in a terrace house in Queensbury Street, Melbourne. It had a very small bathroom on the first landing and a tenant, a Jewish newcomer, living in a tiny room upstairs.

For something to do at lunchtime, I decided to explore the upstairs part of the house. I climbed the steep staircase and found a door ajar. There was the Jewish migrant. His stature was slight and he was casually dressed: a white open neck shirt and plain dark trousers. His brown, straight hair was longish at the front and hung loosely across his forehead.

He was sitting on a small black couch, on one side of the minute room. I invited myself in and sat down on the other side.

I watched him peel, quarter and core a red apple with a small sharp dark handled knife; the peel winding and curling down into a twisted little pile onto his white bread and butter plate.

He then cut the quarters into thin slices and ate them one by one until they were all gone.

I would have stayed longer but my father came looking for me, picked me up and carried me back down into the factory.

The factory contained a large wooden cutting table, a couple of Singer sewing machines, some chairs, a machine for cutting material and a presser.

Moshe stood behind the large wooden cutting table, slowly guiding the machine around the patterns: the pockets, waistband and fly. The material had been folded across a number of times, enabling multiple pairs of trousers to be cut out, simultaneously. When the pieces were ready to be sewn and overlocked, he and Eva set about assembling their first pair. Finally, the trousers were pressed.

Parks Clothing label

They studied the completed product, with a great sense of accomplishment. And so, came about the Manufacturing Business, Parks Clothing.

"*Loz es zeyn mit Muzl.*" "Let it be with good fortune."

Eva and Moshe Berman

That night a pile of pockets and flies, sewn inside out, were brought home and we all sat at the kitchen table turning them the right way around, so that they could be sewn into the trousers the following morning.

THE SECOND FACTORY

The second factory was on the second floor of a building in Little Collins Street, Melbourne, near the corner of Russell Street. It was on the opposite side to the old Post Office.

Factories in that location were later demolished and replaced by a large, dark, modern, high-rise building.

I loved the second factory, right there in the heart of the city, with a thriving little café next door and a TAB in the back lane.

One concrete step off the footpath, the solid, dark wooden door led into a dimly lit stairwell. The sturdy, well-worn wooden stairs went straight up to our factory office, passing two other factories on the ground and first floor levels.

The office was always crammed with packages, full of orders ready to be collected by the carriers who then delivered them to various stores around the city of Melbourne and to some country areas around Victoria.

There was a small desk in a nook facing the stairwell and if I looked over the side, I could see who was coming up the stairs. The desk was piled high, though in an orderly fashion, with paperwork and also an old black telephone.

I sat on the swivel chair at the desk drawing and waiting for the phone to ring so that I could answer it and say, in my best sing song voice, "Parks Cl-ow-th-ing".

Parks Clothing label

A table and four chairs were positioned in a corner of the room where my parents, my uncle, my father's business partner, and my aunt, sat for their coffee breaks and lunch.

It was a vast improvement on Queensbury Street and included a proper kitchen, a bathroom and a separate shower.

The factory area was quite large. A row of machines lined the back and right-hand walls and the wooden cutting table stood on the left side.

It appeared to be a very happy work environment and by all reports it was. My father always maintained a good rapport with his employees and in return they were extremely loyal to him.

I looked forward to the Christmas parties where food and drink were provided and women sang and drank beer. In particular I remember one woman who used to cover her hair with a scarf, I never knew the reason for this, and sang all the old songs, including "My heart belongs to Daddy".

Somewhere along the way my father had become a businessman with trips to Japan, to source the best materials.

The factory was doing extremely well, so a move to larger premises was inevitable.

Eva Berman, Moshe Berman, Etel Kowadlo, Joseph Kowadlo

THE THIRD FACTORY

The third and final factory was in Little Oxford Street, Collingwood. At that time the entire street was dominated by factories, now transformed, into trendy, inner suburban apartments.

It was a massive space with excellent facilities, including a sick room, a showroom and an industrial lift on ground level, which moved rolls and rolls of material upstairs.

During the 1980s, a good friend of my father's, who was a very successful builder, invited him to become a partner in one of his building projects. My father accepted his offer, later selling his share in the manufacturing business, to my uncle.

The venture proved to be a great success. He thoroughly enjoyed the work and had become completely immersed in the building industry and so decided to form his own company, Triubuna Nominees. Two of his friends wanted to be included and became financial partners, my father doing the bulk of the work.

Initially they did very well and after building a fair number of units, all beautifully finished, as Moshe took great pride in his work, there was a recession, which unfortunately caused him to lose a great deal of money.

I don't believe he ever fully recovered from the financial crash and the loss led to his unwanted retirement and my parents' subsequent move to Queensland.

Advertisement on tram

MOVING FORWARD

My parents were eager to get ahead financially and as my father had begun his rigorous education at the age of three, letters they decided to put my age up and sent me off to school when I was nowhere near ready; not emotionally nor in any other way and added to that I spoke no English whatsoever.

My recollection of the first day at school was, sitting on the floor in a crowded, noisy school hall with people moving in every direction until the hall was almost empty, except for a few teachers and me, still sitting there, holding on to a small brown bag, probably containing a rye bread sandwich and a green apple.

Eventually my brother was found and translated some instructions to me, after which I was taken into a classroom.

When I was a child my mother shopped at kosher butchers and delicatessens run by Ultra-Orthodox Jews. I used to stare at them with deep fascination; the way they dressed, behaved and spoke.

Sometimes while waiting for her I stood outside the shop peering in through the window.

It was a world apart. I was Jewish and so were they. I spoke Yiddish and so did they. I knew there was something intrinsically different about them but at the same time there was also something oddly familiar.

Was it some kind of innate recognition, some subconscious memory? Because I had no idea that my grandparent, my great grandparents, uncles and aunts, cousins and my own father lived the same, old worldly life.

When I asked my mother why they dressed the way they did, she explained that it was traditional; the women dressed modestly and the men wore black suits and white shirts and their old worldly styles had barely changed over the years. But I never associated that kind of look with my father. To me he looked particularly modern.

I do recall running down the street towards the old East Melbourne Synagogue to listen to Shofar bloozn, Ram Horn Blowing, on Yom Kippur, The Day of Atonement.

Once I saw my father praying in a Synagogue, wearing his Tullis (prayer shawl), rocking back and forth. I also remember that some Passover celebrations could to be quite long.

He kept a coloured, matt print, which had once hung on the wall, of twenty of the greatest, most learned Rabbis in Israel, from 1013 until 1838, rolled up in a drawer. He used words like, Avereh, transgressor. He listened to and sang songs about God but other than that, synagogue was for weddings and Bar Mitzvahs.

On holidays, we were woken to exhilarating orchestras interpreting Mozart violin sonatas or Tchaikovsky's piano concerto or by the brilliant voice of Jan Peerce, a Jewish operatic tenor and cantor, singing.

"I'll walk with God. I'll take his hand.

I'll talk with God. He'll understand."

Volume turned up full blare, on our record player, which sat nicely in a large nineteen sixties teak cabinet in a corner of our lounge-room. His expansive voice and songs sung are forever incised into my memory.

Eva and Moshe Berman

One may have thought that having sublime euphonic melodies filtering into one's consciousness would be an excellent beginning to the day but contrary to that notion, as a teenager, I yelled, "TURN THAT DOWN!"

We were a family of theatre and filmgoers. Including Yiddish theatre, at the Kadima, which at the time, was in Lygon Street, Carlton. I also remember seeing the Bolshoi Ballet dancing *Swan Lake* and I longed to be a ballerina. Or an actress.

When a play concluded, I charged backstage to talk to the actors, when the audience were permitted to. *The Diary of Anne Frank* was one occasion. The actress who played Anne Frank, was extremely friendly, taking time to talk to me and introduced me to other cast members.

The Savoy Theatre in Russell Street, showed foreign language films in the 1950s, but was sadly closed and demolished in the early 1960s.

It was there I saw Jean Cocteau's film, *Orpheus*, in French, a complicated story with powerful images for a young person, of people walking through mirrors into another world.

THE JEWISH
PROGRESSIVE CENTRE

I never saw my father as a religious man at all and he liked to think of himself as a progressive Jew. In fact, he was one of a group of men who got together regularly, during the 1950s until early 1970. They called themselves The Jewish Progressive Centre.

They were mainly Jews from Poland and most of them ran their own businesses. One was a lecturer at Royal Melbourne Institute of Technology. They were a committed, hardworking, interesting, energetic and intelligent lot, with high ideals who wanted to make the world a better place, their humane outlook and good intentions were sometimes misunderstood by other members of the Jewish community.

During the week they read the political articles in the Australian and Jewish newspapers and once every two weeks, they met at a nominated member's home. Letters in response to the articles, were written and fiery discussions ensued. Occasionally, someone went home upset. At the end of the night, supper was served by one of the wives.

There were numerous events organised during the year such as the Ghetto Commemoration night, picnics and various other social events, including the annual ball.

During the Ghetto Commemoration, six candles were lit for the six million Jews who perished during the Holocaust. We sang Holocaust songs, such as, "*As Brent*," It Burns and "*Shtile Shtile*," Quiet, Quiet. They were songs of loss, pain and despair, of hope, rebirth, courage, determination and the ultimate triumph of the human spirit.

The Partisan song, "*Zog Nit Kein Mol Uz Du geyst dem latstem Veg*," Never Say that this is the Final Road, written by the Jewish poet Hirsh Glik, at the age of twenty-one, was particularly inspirational and was proudly sung, standing, by all who attended the packed to capacity hall.

And for the twentieth anniversary of the Warsaw Ghetto commemoration, the Progressive Centre published a soft cover book, commemorating the occasion, beautifully written and presented. One of the four men who compiled the book was my mother's brother, Joseph Kowadlo.

Jewish Progressive Centre Commemoration Night

Jewish Progressive Centre Commemoration Night

*Abraim Kowadlo, Fera Kowadlo, Morry Walrut, Fela Walrut,
Joseph Kowadlo, Etel Kowadlo, Moshe Berman, Eva Berman*

Anniversary of the Warsaw Uprising book

I remember the annual picnic where The Jewish Progressive Centre, their wives, children and friends, filed onto a hired bus and set off for a day at the beach. Delicious food was shared, either at the wooden tables on site or on blankets laid out on the rough, grassy area behind the beach.

We played volleyball, shuttlecock, had egg and spoon, running, and swimming races. Moshe was a strong swimmer and came first in freestyle and Eva's brother Joseph, won the breaststroke. No great feat, as they were the only two competitors. Swimming not featuring very highly on the list of priorities at the Jewish Progressive Centre.

There was also a "Best Leg competition".

A large blanket was attached to the two shuttlecock posts and the women lined up behind the blanket, showing only legs below their bathers.

No one knew to whom the legs belonged and everyone wanted their say as to which legs were the best. There were noisy disagreements but a lone adjudicator, had the final say and he deemed that Etel, Josephs wife, had the best legs. She happily accepted the accolade.

Jewish Progressive Centre Picnic.
Front: Fela Walrut. Left: Eva Berman

Jewish Progressive Centre Picnic

WEEKENDS

At about two or three years old, I attended a Jewish Kindergarten. At Primary level, a Jewish school on Sunday mornings and when I was at High school, it included, Wednesday after school. All with my first cousin, Hannah.

Getting there on time on Sundays was usually a struggle, as nobody wanted to get out of bed early on Sunday.

We learnt to read and write Yiddish, studied Jewish History and a little literature.

In class the teacher's voice drifted in and out of my consciousness and every now and again I'd look at his face, the way his mouth moved as he spoke, his eyes, how animated or otherwise he was, without taking too much notice of what he was saying.

Hannah Kowadlo, Esther Berman

Esther Berman, Hannah Kowadlo

*Hannah Kowadlo second row, second from left,
Esther Berman, back row, third from right*

As the class progressed, I thought about what I was going to do that afternoon, who was coming over to our place and wondered whether or not my father would be picking us up on time, because we often had to stand outside the school building, waiting for him.

Some of the information from Yiddish school must have sunk in because I still know a bit of history; I write Yiddish without too much trouble and with a little effort I can still read Yiddish.

There were of course a few memorable lessons; one was a debate about the pogroms inflicted upon Jews during the Spanish Inquisition, when Jewish people were forced to convert to Christianity or they would be abused, expelled from the country, or killed.

Hannah Kowadlo, Esther Berman

Some converted, others pretended to convert and then practised Judaism secretly but there were those who chose to die for their faith.

We were asked to take sides: die for your religion or practise secretly thereby continuing the faith.

Initially, I leaned towards the idealistic option, like Daniel, in the lion's den. Daniel who was prepared to die rather than stop praying to God. In the sixth Century BC during the reign of King Darius the Mede, a law was passed, that for thirty days, no-body was allowed to pray except to King Darius. But the prophet Daniel refused to give up his commitment to God and continued to pray. Therefore, the administrators of the land forced the King's hand and Daniel was placed into the lion's den.

However, the teacher's argument was a compelling one. His position was that if every Jew died for their religion there would be no Jewish religion left to follow.

Most Sunday afternoons, relatives or friends came to our home for afternoon tea, often staying on for dinner.

The children played outside for hours, either rollerskating or rolling down our incredibly steep hill in billycarts made, out of old wooden boxes, with a stick inserted through the middle, which served as a steering wheel, made by my very smart brother, who did incredibly difficult crossword puzzles at an early age, played the piano and sang in a rock band with a few of his school friends, even performing in a competition on television and gaining first place. As an adult he completely rebuilt a beat-up old Chevy, from scratch, turning it into an immaculate vehicle. His academic gifts were, for a time, put into storage.

My cousin Hannah tenaciously tried to master the art of roller-skating but eventually, frustrated and hurt by her innumerable falls, she tied a pillow around her bottom to lessen the pain when impacting the ground.

Hannah and I were complete opposites in appearance. She had an olive complexion, black curly hair and brown eyes and I was very pale with straight light blonde hair and green eyes.

We had great fun pretending that we were twins. People tended to believe us after we told them that I looked like our mother, who was fair and that she looked like our father who was dark. Perhaps they were just humouring us. Either way, most people said that there was something similar about us.

During the Christmas holidays, we jumped, twisted, turned, sat and sprung back into an upright position on the trampolines, at the Rosebud foreshore.

Rachel Becker, Sophie Zemel, Etel Kowadlo, Joseph Kowadlo, Jacob Zemel, Moshe Berman, Charles Becker

"Time's up," the trampoline attended said, and we got off the trampoline.

"We're twins you know," I said to him.

"Yes," he said, tongue in cheek, "I can see the resemblance."

We laughed and began our slow walk back to our holiday house, in McCrae.

We derived immeasurable joy out of mimicking and sending up our parents and discussing suitable Australian names for ourselves, neither of us having been too keen on our distinctly Jewish names.

"My father calls factory, FA-C-TRE." I said unfurling my arms to accentuate the word.

"FA-C-TRE."

"Fact-re, Fact-re. Let's go to the Fact-re." Hannah laughingly repeated.

"I don't want to be called Esther. I'd rather have an Australian name."

"Hannah, who has a name like Hannah? I hate my name."

"What would you call yourself?"

"I like Joy or Joan. I think I'll call myself Joan. That's an Australian name. Don't call me anything else. Joan is my name now."

"I will.......call myself.... Maureen. That sounds really Australian."

But I did not realise that, at that point, for her, the name change was absolute.

I stopped to examine some of the many seashells, washed up onto the sand but Hannah kept on walking.

She was quite some distance ahead so I began running and shouting, "Hannah, Hannah! Wait for me!" She refused to stop or even to turn around. I thought she must have been deaf. When I finally caught up, I asked her why she didn't wait for me. She replied, "My name isn't Hannah, it's Joan." "But nobody heard," I said. "Two people just walked past."

We did not attend the same primary school although for a couple of years we did go to the same high school.

Back: Hannah Dunne (Kowadlo), Esther Naylor (Berman). Front: Julian Dunne, Zoe Naylor

At high school, having been tempted by the enticing lunchtime aromas emanating from our school canteen, we walked home to Hannah's place for lunch with cream buns. They had all been attractively lined up on a tray, on the canteen counter.

Hannah ate hers immediately so that her mother, who always told us to leave our giggles at the door when we came home for lunch, would not know she had bought one. I on the other hand kept mine until we walked back to school.

The sight of me utterly enjoying my delectable pastry proved too much for Hannah, a lover of cream buns, so she took a few well aimed swipes at the cream inside my bun, causing squeals of hilarity and me to defend my tasty treat, to the end.

Some of our childhood was spent outside climbing and sitting on the gnarled branches of our old pear tree, eating pears and pretending to be in Enid Blyton's Faraway Tree, travelling to distant lands.

"Look at me. Look at me! I'm sitting in a funny old pear tree," I said.

"Look at me. Look at me! I'm throwing my core on the ground for all to see," Hannah said, hurling her core. We laughed and climbed up as far as we could so that we could.

"Listen." I said, drawing in breath. "I can hear singing."

We both, feigned listening.

"Me too."

"People singing to one another."

"And look the animals, they're singing too."

"What beautiful music."

"Look people are wearing such bright clothes!"

"So are the animals."

"Mar...vell...ous!"

"My name is Esther!" I sang.

She sung, "My name is Hannah!"

"Can someone come and help me?" Michael yelled, as he dug an enormous square in the backyard, finally hammering in a long stick near the inner edge. We climbed down from the tree, and got into the centre of the dug-out square.

"Where are we going?" we asked.

"To a land where even children drive spectacular cars. PREPARE TO LAUNCH!"

We also created different characters for ourselves and made up dance steps to perform in front of anyone who cared to watch.

"Oh, why do I always have to be the boy?" she complained as I issued instructions on how to best facilitate my leap into the air with her standing behind me, her hands around my hips.

During adolescence, through to adulthood, we spent a great deal of our leisure time at the beach, walking, talking, laughing and endlessly sunbaking until Hannah was black and I was the colour of milk chocolate.

I was one of her two bridesmaids. We socialised, talked on the phone, spent warm Christmas days cooking [separately, as Hannah would never allow anyone to interfere, when she was cooking] and feasting on delicious dinners; our families holidayed together and her son and my daughter went to the same kindergarten.

Over the years we maintained a genuine interest in each other's activities and pursuits even though at times, we did not see each other. Naturally, there were disagreements and when we were young there was even one case of very, very serious hair pulling, but they were never left unresolved.

One morning when Hannah was about fourteen, my mother came into my bedroom and was astonished to find her asleep at the other end of my bed. The night before she had run away from home and had taken refuge at our place. She snuck in through my bedroom window and swore me to secrecy.

Zoe Naylor, Julian Dunne, Hannah Dunne

At eighteen Hannah moved in with us for good. She even bought a little dog, Bim, something she would never have been allowed to do at home. She stayed until the day of her marriage.

"Dad, Robin just proposed to me. What do you think I should do?" Her father's eyes lit up. He beamed.

"I can't tell you that!"

Hannah Dunne, Esther Berman

We were sitting around our white Laminex, rectangular kitchen table, drinking tea; in the three-bedroom apartment my parents had rented as a stopgap, after selling our house in a hilly, picturesque suburb of Melbourne and buying one in North Caulfield, closer to their friends and relatives. Hannah had moved into the third bedroom.

"Go on," she persisted, "What do you think?"

He laughed, "You have to decide for yourself. It's your decision, not mine."

"Please Dad, please, tell me."

It was obvious that he could hardly contain his emotions and probably wanted to yell, "Yes, for sure, marry him! I like him very much." But he held back.

I said, "Just do it! Do it if you love him!"

She was radiant but strangely, even though she knew that her father was very fond of her boyfriend, she still wanted to hear him say that he approved of her marriage.

We already knew what her answer would be. No encouragement needed.

She saw me sitting on the sand, at St. Kilda beach, a place we called Little Jerusalem, where Jewish teenagers hung out during the hot summer months in Melbourne.

It was a small stretch of grass and the beach beyond it, alongside Jacka Boulevard, behind the Esplanade, near the Kiosk where we bought our ice creams and icy poles. Traffic zooming. Though it cannot be compared to the ultra-busy traffic, powering along that road today.

I was lazily leaning back onto the one who was to become her husband, known to her, only casually then. He was tilted back, weight on both arms outstretched behind him, palms flat, turning away from his body and planted in the sand, his knees drawn up and feet in the sand, legs open at an angle, I was wedged in between his open legs, facing outwards, my knees also pulled up, my toes wriggling in the warm sand, with both of my arms casually resting on both of his knees. We were basking in the sun, talking.

She stood to the right in front of us, closer to the water; head thoughtfully inclined to the side, took a mental snap shot and liked the image generated. Knowing that the relationship between me, and my fellow "loller", was one of camaraderie, she said to herself, "Mm... mm, I think I'll have him." And that I reflect was the beginning of their romance.

And later, in her thirties, with that same tenacious spirit she used to master the skill of roller-skating she bravely wrestled the beast, wanting above all to see her children grow into adulthood. But the cancer edged its way back, gaining ground, ravaging her and was the final victor.

"She doesn't understand," she once said, alluding to her state of health. It was to a friend of hers and in my presence.

"I do understand," I said. "Of course, I do." But I didn't and I wouldn't.

Another night, she had come to see me in an acting performance and I was delighted to see her there. She was very tired as she had just been to the opening of an art exhibition. She said that she had made a special effort to look good because she did not want people to see her only as a cancer sufferer.

Hannah did look good. She was very fashionably dressed in a below the knee grey coat; grey being the in colour that season and she was very beautiful with masses of black wavy hair, loosely nudging her shoulders.

She said, "I wouldn't have come if it hadn't been you."

When on my second last visit to the hospital I saw a book about dying on her bedside table, I was determined that I was not going to cry. So, with every bit of self-control I could muster, I bound up my emotions so tightly that all Hannah saw was a mass of high voltage tension.

I was thrilled to see her so much better on my next visit to the hospital. She was sitting up in bed crocheting. And I still believed that she would live.

But when, shortly after my hospital visit, in a phone conversation she told me that she could no longer make decisions for herself, my emotions battered their way through into deep, deep wails, deep wails of sorrow.

Never forgotten Hannah, never ever forgotten.

Hannah Dunne

CHRISTMAS AT
THE BEACH

Every Christmas holidays our family drove to the beach, where we rented a house for two and sometimes three weeks.

Christmas was a massive event when I was a child. For me the build-up to it was electric. At primary school we sang Christmas carols and made colourful decorations and cards.

Multitudes of lights and colourful decorations were displayed everywhere; in the street, inside and outside shops and department stores, The Salvation Army gathered in groups, singing, clapping tambourines and playing their trumpets. Everyone crowded into town to see the famous Myer Melbourne windows, which beautifully depicted the story of Christmas, scene by scene. Presents and cards, wishing happiness to all were exchanged. It was very festive.

My school friends discussed who would be attending their Christmas dinners and recounted humorous stories of the previous year's festivities. They talked excitedly about the delicious meal they were going to eat and of course, the presents they hoped to receive from their families and from "Father Christmas", now usually referred to as Santa Claus, and the gifts they were buying or making for members of their own families. I felt left out.

So once while holidaying at the beach, my brother and I decided to hang our pillowcases up on hooks to see what Santa would bring for us.

Our parents were amused.

"What are you doing?" they asked.

"We're hanging our pillowcases up so that Father Christmas can fill them with presents while we're asleep because that's what he does the night before Christmas."

My father laughed, "But Father Christmas does not come to Jewish children."

I said, "He might. You don't know that. We can try it anyway."

"Don't be silly Esther, he's not coming."

We woke up early the next morning and eagerly ran to our hanging pillowcases. They were empty. Not even an orange. Our disappointment was enormous but our parents, while perhaps sympathetic, said, "But why are you so upset? You knew Father Christmas did not bring presents to Jewish children."

I experienced my first Christmas celebrations, except for those factory Christmas parties, when I was married and invited to my husband's family for Christmas dinner. I was completely taken with it.

PASSOVER IN AUSTRALIA

There is an all pervasive warmth in the brightly lit, large well-arranged lounge-room, where thirteen relaxed and happy people sat comfortably around a teak rectangular table, now covered by a crisp white tablecloth, eating the first course of their Passover meal.

A large impressionistic oil painting of Melbourne in the rain, a landscape and a painting of an orange terrace house, hang on the pale walls surrounding them.

Two brightly burning candles in golden candle holders, a few photos of children, grandchildren, deceased family members and some kitschy ornaments are placed in a minimalistic fashion on the long sleek, handmade and perfectly constructed, sixties sideboard.

Eva Berman, Zoe Naylor, Moshe Berman, Tania Berman, Simon Berman, Abram Kowadlo

Tania Berman, Michael Berman, Simon Berman, Zoe Naylor

Conversation flows. There are four generations here; two of Eva's uncles, who are brothers, their wives, Eva and Moshe, my brother, his wife, son and daughter, aged six and seven, my husband Tim, and my daughter, Zoe eight years old, and myself.

The table is splendidly set with fine white, light blue delicately patterned china, sparkling silver cutlery, an array of dishes containing delectable dips, including chopped liver, various vegetables, salads and of course, Matzos.

There is also an empty silver platter, except for the tiny remnant of a cooked carrot, on which the gefilte fish was presented.

The younger, more- portly of the grey-haired uncles, a wonderfully jovial fellow, complements Eva on her excellent cooking.

He has both arms loosely folded around his large round belly.

"The fish Eva, absolutely delicious, *azoy gut!*" So good!

He turns his head towards his Russian born wife, who asked,

"Is it so different to mine?"

Assuring her, he says, "Yours my dear is always good of course."

BALANCING

*Moshe Berman, Abram Kowadlo, Simon Berman, Zoe Naylor,
Fera Kowadlo, Tania Berman, Tim Naylor. Back row: Elaine Berman*

Fera Kowadlo, Tania Berman, Tim Naylor, Zoe Naylor

"But Eva, this time the fish, mm-mm, *azoy geshmuk!*"
"So tasty."

Eva is obviously delighted by his appreciation and removing the empty plates from the table says,

"I'm so glad you enjoyed it. Really, was it so good?"

"*Avade Eva.*" "Of course, Eva," Moshe adds, getting up from the table.

"*Meyn weib can auch kochn.*" "My wife can also cook."

Wanting to move towards her, he accidentally overturns an almost empty, glass of water. He begins mopping the water up with his serviette. Eva goes back to help.

CLEANING

I was sick in bed and my mother came to our house to take care of me. It was an extremely hot day.

My husband had decided to take our daughter, who was under the age of two, out for the afternoon.

Our home was a large red brick Victorian place and my mother decided it would be nice to clean the kitchen for me while I slept.

I woke up to the sound of voices somewhere in the house and decided to get up and see who it was.

There, in the kitchen, was my mother, a very large breasted woman, encased in this fierce, skin coloured, waist length contraption, with tiny multiple hooks running up the back, which was obviously the forerunner to the modern day bustier. It did look like a top.

Zoe Naylor, Eva Berman

Eva Berman, Nicholas Naylor, Moshe Berman

She was completely unconcerned about her appearance.

The owner of the house was visiting and they were both sitting at our small dark varnished table, having a nice cup of tea and what appeared to be a most engrossing conversation.

She looked up at me when I came into the room and said, "Oh Esther, you're awake. How do you feel?"

"You're in your bra Mum," I said.

She had taken her top off due to the heat.

"So, what?"

"Greg's here."

"How does he know this is my bra? It might be a top for all he knows."

"He can see."

"No, I didn't know," said Greg, not looking in our direction.

QUEENSLAND
The Beginning

I heard a loud crash, then "Oh no!" It was silent for a moment and then, "I loved that, that was my favourite dish."

When I came in from the balcony, Eva was looking down in dismay at her shattered light blue and grey casserole dish and a kilo of half cooked chicken wings in a pool of marinade, splattered across the floor.

The dish had slipped out of her hands when she was attempting, with the help of a tea towel, to take it out of the oven, so that she could turn the wings over.

Eva Berman

Nicholas Naylor

We picked up all the pieces and cleaned the floor but I could see that she was still very upset.

She seemed so vulnerable today. Something had changed. Last night at the Casino, while we were having dinner, she unexpectedly raised her glass of red wine and confidently made a beautiful toast to me, thanking me for being her daughter. But today she was unsure somehow.

I told her not to worry about anything and that tonight we would be having pizza for dinner.

Moshe's questions and comments about what happened to the dinner, I knew, were not going to be very helpful so, I went across the road to the oval where he and Nick were playing a game of cricket.

I described, in detail, what had just taken place and firmly instructed him not to mention a word about it to Eva.

The next morning, I actually asked her if he had. She said no. I found it remarkable as I imagine he would have found not commenting very difficult indeed.

We returned to the apartment and Nick moved the small, white circular table over to one end of the balcony and placed four, blue and white, overlapping strapped, folding chairs, around it and a white tablecloth on top.

We bought a variety of pizzas ranging from a margarita to a one with the lot, and a bottle of red wine and my son became the waiter for the night; continuously bringing us hot pizza from the oven.

It was a beautiful hot summer's night. We sat outside on the balcony with the bright lights of Surfers Paradise in the distance, talking and laughing for more than a couple of hours. It was the perfect conclusion to our summer holiday but it was also the emergence of a very cruel and ugly disease, Alzheimer's.

LATER VISITS

"Do you speak Yiddish?" "No, I don't," Nick says.
"What, you don't speak Yiddish? Shame on you, how can that be?"

"I never learnt it."

"Why that's terrible. You should be ashamed of yourself."

My son was upset. He certainly did not expect his grandmother to forget who he was. She adored him and it was always a special occasion for her, whenever he was around. But for approximately ten years, she only saw him once or twice a year, depending on how often we went to Queensland.

She remembered him as a young boy but he had grown to six feet one inch, and was twenty-one years old.

On another occasion my parents picked me up from the airport; I was alone. I hadn't seen them for six months. My mother recognised me immediately but later that night, as I lay in bed, I listened impassively to the conversation between my parents.

"Who is the woman in the bedroom, Moshe?"

"That's Esther, your daughter."

"That's Esther? *Bist du mashiga?*" Are you crazy?

"That's Esther I tell you."

"The woman in the bedroom is not my daughter."

EVA'S COUSIN ANGE

I was getting ready to go for my morning walk on the beach when I heard, "Are you Ange?"

What? Ange died in a concentration camp years ago. Who are you calling Ange?

"Come on girl."

"Do you mean me?" I call out from the bathroom.

"Oh, I must have had a dream. It seemed so real to me. Esther had brownish hair and olive skin."

I did look like that for a while.

"Remember the story 'My Brother's name is Nicholas Jack' about Nickie?" I say, trying to get her back to reality.

"Nicholas Jack it's your birthday today and there's such a lot I'd like to say."

"Yes, oh yes. But what's that got to do with me being in Queensland?"

"Shh... be quiet. Stop talking about it. Dad will lose his temper with you."

He had been known to yell at her for going on the way she does and she was simply fuelling the situation by continuing.

"Oh, who cares? Do you really think I take that much notice about all the things he says?"

She continues,

"These were all my mother's things." She points to the paintings, tablecloth and a few other items around the room.

"Your mother perished in Europe during the War and you came to this country penniless. Don't say they were your mother's things," my father interjects.

"I'll say it if I want to. I believe it and I'll die believing it."

He simply gives up. He's been through this scenario many times.

So, I went into the story about coming to Australia and all the houses she'd lived in and when she got her furniture and paintings.

She remembered most of it.

It seemed to be going well. I said, "You've been overcome with a sudden attack of Mishigas" – the crazies. She laughed.

"But look Esther, our family has been in Australia for all these years. How is it that I haven't seen you for such a long time?" She started up again.

"You have seen me. I come here twice or three times a year and stay for two weeks or so. You've just forgotten. You've got the forgetting disease."

She also found that very amusing. At least she still had her sense of humour. Laugh or go under.

Nicholas Naylor, Eva Berman

LETTERBOXES

My father, Moshe, is in his front garden inspecting the row of letterboxes. There are eight cream brick apartments in the block with eight letterboxes built into the low brick fence. None of them are locked and when it's windy the metal doors clang relentlessly as they open and close, open and close.

It has been windy all week and yesterday Moshe collected a number of twigs, which he pushed through the small metal loops used for inserting the locks. He took the rest upstairs and set them aside for future use if needed.

Because of the wind, however, many of the twigs had fallen out and been swept away. So, he returned upstairs to collect the remaining twigs. Unfortunately, their whereabouts eluded him.

He searched everywhere for the misplaced twigs, muttering,

"Where are those sticks? Where are those sticks?"

Finally, he asked Eva, "*Eva, wu zanen di shtekalech?*" "Eva, where are those twigs?"

She stopped reading and raised her head, stared at him and said,

"*Welcher shtekalech?*" "What kind of twigs?"

He said, "*Du veyst di shtechalech fun nachtnn.*" "You know the twigs from yesterday."

Exasperated, because he constantly involved her in his tiresome searches, she says,

"*Ich hab zey arein gesetst in dreyd zolen vuxn.*"

"I stuck them in the ground so that they'd grow!"

There is a moment between them but then, quite unperturbed, he continues his search until he finally locates the missing twigs.

He says, "You know, if my father was alive, he would never have allowed this marriage." He meant that she would not have been religious enough for his family.

Eva, probably hurt, but with a quick wave of her hand says, "Oh, your father. Do you think I care about that?" He takes his sticks downstairs. Intrigued, Eva steps out onto the balcony and watches Moshe conscientiously, re-insert the twigs into the clanging...clanging letter-boxes. He looks up, catching her eye.

MAKING LATKES

My daughter, son and I were sitting around the kitchen table with empty plates in front of us, waiting for my mother to finish making the latkes. The smell was alluring and we were eager to get stuck into them.

My father stood at the stove next to her, overseeing the frying. He knew that she was very sensitive about people interfering when she was cooking but he could not keep his comments to himself.

"*Mach a bisl braunyer Eva,*" he says. "Let them brown a little more."

"*Vos shteyst di du azoi Moshe? Gehst awek tzu nisht. Du kanst machn beser?*" "Why are you standing here like that Moshe? Are you going away or not? Can you do any better?"

"*Yo, es miz zeyn mer up gebrent.*" "Yes, it must be a little more brown."

"Leave her alone." "Give her a break." "Let her do it her way." "Come over here Moshe." We all said simultaneously.

Realizing that he was outnumbered, he forced himself away from his post and sat down at the table with us.

He called out.

"Eva, be so kind as to give us a little more sugar."

"I'll look for it," she said.

Zoe, Esther and Nicholas. Front: Samuel Krasna.

He turned to me and said quietly,

"Mum probably put it away. Maybe she put it in the fridge."

She yelled back,

"Maybe I put it in the bed."

PHOTOS

"But I don't know you. Who are you?" Eva said without any warning, as we sat chatting on her large sunny first floor balcony. I was sitting on the two-seater floral high back, curved couch, my feet up. She sat on a white straight plastic, fold up chair.

"I don't recognise the face."

"I'm Esther, your daughter," I said.

"You're Esther? But your face...I don't recognise it!" She looked distressed.

I said nothing; two breaths in, two breaths out.

No expression on my face.

Then I said, "Wait for a second and I'll show you the photos. Let's go through them. It will all come back to you."

I went inside and got the old shoebox from under the dressing table in her bedroom. It was filled with photos from the past, each with their own story, their own time, place and feeling. We went through them all one by one. I showed her one of me holding my daughter just after she was born. We were sitting on the white wooden slatted chair my father had made years before.

"That's me with Zoë. Do you see the resemblance?" I said.

I looked tired in the photo but she answered, "Yes, maybe," pausing for a moment, "a little bit."

She remembered all of her friends and then we came across one of me siting on someone's veranda when I was twenty-one. I was overseas at the time. My face was full and suntanned and my hair, long and blonde. I handed her the photo and said,

"Look who's that? Do you recognise her?"

She looked, knowingly, lovingly, slowly nodding her head, a little smile on her face, "Yes, that's Esther."

GIVE ME YOUR MONEY

It was a hot November morning as Moshe and Eva, now in their eighties, took some money out of the automatic teller machine, in the busy Broadbeach mall.

A robust tan, young woman dressed in a light, short skirt, a colourful blouse and sandals, suddenly appeared before them, as they turned to leave the machine.

"Give me your money!" she commanded in a most authoritative tone.

"No! I will not give you my money," Moshe immediately responded; sounding more authoritative than his would-be assailant.

Taken aback by his unexpected audacity she faded back into the crowd, no doubt looking for her next victim.

"Did you tell Nickie?" Moshe asked me.

"Yes, I did," I said.

"What did he say?"

"He was impressed."

My father chuckled.

MELBOURNE

Moshe said, after one of my visits, that he didn't think he could go back to cooking again. I wasn't sure if he was serious or if he was just being complimentary, as I did most of the cooking when I stayed with them.

I had been begging him to come back to Melbourne and said that I didn't know when I could return to Queensland, as I was just starting a new job.

I usually spoke to my parents on the phone once a week but sometimes more often. It was our second last conversation and my father was sounding a bit tired.

I said, "I'm looking for an apartment for you. You have to come back to Melbourne."

Day and night, I had scoured real estate on the internet looking for places for them. Places for me. Places for me and them. My search took me beyond the city into country areas as I envisioned living with them, in the same house. The adjustment would have been major but I allowed my imagination to play with the possibility.

He said, "*Dos is nischt azoy wazne. Dos iz nicht azoi wazne.*"

"That is not so important. That is not so important." He did sound a bit weary but there was no sense of foreboding.

THE PHONE CALL

A few days later, a friend of his rang me, "I think there's something wrong with Moshe. He didn't sound right."

I rang my parents immediately and tried to talk to Moshe but he kept repeating, "Oh Esther, Oh Esther, Oh Esther, Oh Esther." My heart pounded. I was terrified.

I hung up the phone and rang the Broadbeach Police Station, which is in the same street, just a short walk away. I told them about my parents' situation and that they had no family in Queensland. I asked if they could go and check on them.

They rang back and said that they had called an ambulance. I telephoned my parents and spoke to my mother. I had to tell her what to expect and I hoped that she would remember my words.

I said, "Mum go and open the front door, an ambulance is coming. I'll wait here while you do it." She said, "Alright."

She came back to the phone.

"Dad's in a bad way."

She said, "I know. What can I do about it?"

The ambulance arrived and I spoke to the Paramedic, who told me which hospital they would be going to.

I booked the next flight to Queensland and packed my bag.

THE APARTMENT

I unlocked the door to the apartment and walked in.

Their presence was very strong. The apartment had a sense of tragic emptiness. It hung in the air. It was in every breath I took as I moved slowly into the lounge-room and across to the kitchen.

I opened the food cupboard. Almost empty. I went to the fridge. Inside, on the top shelf, a half-opened tin of sardines in tomato sauce. The sauce looked thick and was dark red in colour. Oh God, how long has that been there? Did Moshe just lose interest in the sardines or did he feel too weak to continue opening the tin?

There were also a couple of old pieces of fruit. I felt sick to the core. Normally, they never would have left anything like that. I closed the fridge door.

To the right, on top of the stove was a stainless-steel pot with a long thin handle, containing dried out, cooked Weet-Bix. Had he forgotten what to do with them? When had they ever cooked Weet-Bix? Was there nothing left to eat in the house? I was shaking.

Obviously, they were unable to go out shopping. Eva could not shop by herself any more. She was completely dependent on Moshe. Heartbreaking. But I told myself that I could not cry right now. I had to go to the hospital.

THE HOSPITAL

My father was lying in bed and my mother sat on a chair very close to him. They were huddled together in conversation when the nurse showed me in.

Moshe's eyes lit up when he saw me. He must have been so relieved to know that there was someone to look after Eva. She had been sitting at his bedside all night. The staff knew of her condition and that he was her caregiver but they didn't know what to do with her.

The doctor came in to examine Moshe and after I introduced myself to him, he delivered his prognosis.

"He has a brain tumour and he's dying."

His brain had swollen and that was the reason he was unable to utter any words but, "Oh, Esther." They would give him steroids to relieve the swelling.

LET'S GO TO AMERICA

"Hey Moshe, what do you think? Do you want to go to America? It's no good here. What do you say? Will we travel to America? I've got a *groshen in beytle*". "I've got some coins in my handbag."

"Are you cold," she asks continuously, gently rubbing his chest, completely fixated on his body temperature. He shakes his head,

"No."

A few minutes later and pointing to his chest,

"Aren't you cold here?"

This time he doesn't answer.

I say, "He's already said he isn't."

She says, "Well can't he say it again? I hate it when he doesn't answer me. It's as if I'm already dead." "Dad, are you too tired to talk?" He nods.

Trying to sound light-hearted I say, "What happens when you get other visitors and you have to talk?" There's no reply.

She says, "They'll say, oh that Moshe he can't even talk."

No movement or emotion.

She had no idea that he was so close to death and by the end of next week we'd be bringing his body back to Melbourne.

She says,

"*Du vilst groysn apple Moshe?*" "Do you want a large apple Moshe?"

She waits a few seconds and then, "In a minute he'll get up and do a Zaddik tentsl." A dance of the wise men.

He's still unresponsive and she's getting scared.

"What's happening Moshe, do you want to get up and dressed now? Are we going home or what are we doing?"

He simply looked at her, knowing that she did not understand the situation. But he had no energy for explanations.

My father and I had developed an understanding which was not defined by words. His face signalled to me somehow. I knew exactly what he meant even though his expression hardly altered.

My daughter Zoe rang Moshe from Melbourne.

I handed him the phone and left the room to sit in the passage.

I could see him through the large window; an eighty-seven-year-old man, sitting on his hospital bed, two skinny legs dangling over the side of the bed.

He held the phone close to his right ear, listening intently to his granddaughter's voice. His composed face twisted with emotion. Tears filled his eyes and trickled down his cheeks.

"What were you saying to him?" I asked her later.

"I was just telling him how concerned I was about him and that I hoped he would be alright."

That was the first and last time I ever saw my father cry.

THE GETAWAY

His clothes were in the small metal, bedside cabinet. He takes them all out carefully and slowly dresses himself. Removes a white plastic bag from the top drawer and packs the rest of his belongings into it.

He begins walking clumsily down the hospital passage and out of the building.

Some of the nurses are sitting in the rectangular nurses' station chatting. A table covered with chocolates, for sale, stands next to the counter and one of the nurses is using the computer.

They do not notice him at first. They think he is just one of the visitors leaving. But then one of them suddenly realises who it is and chases him down the corridor. She takes hold of him and brings him back into his room. Leaves him sitting on the bed.

The door is shut. The passage closed off. There is no escape.

"Where did you think you were going? You had no money," I asked him when I found out what had happened. He just sat on his bed looking back at me, a slight smile on his face.

A MEETING IS HELD

A liaison officer came to the hospital, from the Palliative Centre across the road, to organise a meeting with me and a couple of the nurses, in regards to palliative care for my father.

She decided to hold the meeting in my father's room and I did not object. She asked everyone to bring in a chair. The room was crowded.

There were more people than I had anticipated. We sat in two rows opposite each other. My mother and father were to the side, near my father's bed, somewhat isolated from the group.

The liaison officer began speaking. She gave me a couple of options. Either to take my father home and receive some help from the team there, or send him upstairs to the palliative care ward.

I looked over at my parents; my mother confused, uncertain. My father dismayed.

I had definitely made a mistake, having the meeting in his room with both of them present. We were making plans for the rest of my father's life without giving him any say in it, at all. As if he was not even there. I knew very well how he would have hated that and I thoroughly regret having done it.

Luckily, the meeting did not last long. Ultimately, I did not believe that I would be able to look after a dying man and a woman with Alzheimer's all by myself, at night.

The nurses were going to try and move him upstairs to the palliative ward and I believed that to be the best option.

I desperately wanted to get my parents back to Melbourne so that they could have more of their loved ones around them. And that is where the air ambulance came in.

AMBULANCE NEEDED

I had secretly organised the air ambulance to come and take my father back to Melbourne because the staff at the hospital were determined not to let him leave. They said he was dying. Insisting that it was not safe for him to travel. How unsafe could it be? As they said, he was dying.

They had stopped a previous attempt of mine to get both of my parents onto a flight. My brother was waiting in Melbourne, ready to pick us up at the airport. The tickets were booked and we were all set to go. But at the last minute they changed their minds.

I needed assistance to get them both onto the plane.

Initially, Moshe seemed happy about returning to Melbourne. He was looking forward to celebrating my birthday with the rest of the family. But later, I could see that he was feeling a little anxious about it.

I finally said, "Just tell me if you don't want to go."

"I don't want to go," he whispered. There was silence and that was it.

GET YOU TONIGHT

They stood outside in the ward.
And later in his room.

"We'll get you tonight," whispered the hospital orderly, as he moved him onto the bed.

What was that? What did he say? Am I actually hearing that correctly? We'll get you tonight? Why? Why did he say that?

Moshe was completely vulnerable. He had a brain tumour and was in no state to argue.

When we came to the hospital the next day, he had been moved into another ward.

He sat on a chair slumped on an angle, part of him leaning on the bed and part propped up on the hospital chair, his eyes bulging. His head had fallen across his right shoulder. A vacant expression on his face.

"What did they do to you?" I asked horrified.

He stared back.

The nurse stood listening, her face tomato red.

"I didn't do anything," she said defensively.

"What's happened to him? Look at him," I said.

But she had no answer.

I started rubbing his back and tried to straighten him up. With Eva's help we sat him up and somehow managed to get him back onto the bed.

His face began to relax a little.

"They are never going to do that to you again," I said.

He stared.

But what did I know.

My father was a diabetic and needed to stabilise his blood sugar levels by eating small meals throughout the day, even if it was only a dry biscuit for morning and afternoon tea. But no amount of talking on my part could convince the hospital staff to provide this sustenance for him.

He was moved out of his private room, into a large orthopaedic ward, with many beds on either side of the room. It did not seem to be an appropriate place for him.

A nurse offered him a bed upstairs in the palliative ward, which would have been ideal, but she withdrew the offer the same day without giving any explanation.

I was aware of his anxiety concerning the Palliative Care centre across the road. He stared at me in horror as they informed me of their decision to send him there. He knew that would be the end. There was no coming back. Not from there.

The night before my brother and his son had come from Adelaide, and my son, from Melbourne, to see Moshe. We sat surrounding his bed. He was sitting up, pillows behind him and covered with a blanket, more alert than usual, although I don't think he was aware of how many of us there were. I told him who was present and he was very pleased.

In turn my brother and his son went over and spoke to him. He acknowledged them, tightly squeezing their hands. Nick then hugged him, emotional. He said, "Hello Moshe."

Returning the next day, we found his bed empty. I was directed to the transit area where patients waited to be transported out of the hospital by ambulance.

He was lying unattended in a wheelchair in the middle of a large, unpleasant smelling room, empty except for two nurses having a social conversation, one behind a counter and the other in front of it.

My father was in a terrible condition, completely dehydrated and unable to speak.

I yelled, "This man is a human being! This man is my father!"

The Indian nurse standing closest to him said, "Will I make him a drink?"

"Yes, please do."

I was exasperated by the complete lack of interest in someone so obviously ill.

She raised the back of his chair so that he was in a sitting position, then made him a cup of white tea with one sugar.

I held the cup next to his mouth and he grasped it wildly with both hands, gulping down the tea like someone who had not had anything to drink for days.

We sat talking to him until the ambulance arrived. I told him that I had tried my best to keep him at the hospital but that all my attempts had been unsuccessful.

Eva and I walked across the busy road to the Palliative Care Centre while Moshe was transferred by ambulance.

His double room felt warm and was nice and clean. It was partitioned partly by a wall and the rest with a green curtain pulled across. A nurse showed me to the kitchen and said we could help ourselves to anything there. I got some green and red jelly out of the fridge and brought a bowl of it to my father. He allowed me to feed him and seemed to enjoy eating it.

So brave and independent right up until the end. He had never allowed himself to be fed by anyone, always insisting on feeding himself, no matter how long it took him. Except for this one time, this last time, with the raspberry and lime jelly.

That night was the only time he ever had morphine for the pain. He was in agony. I covered his head with both of my hands and held them there until he settled a little.

I left the room to ring my daughter and then we went home.

"But I don't want to leave my husband," my mother implored. Her last words as we left the hospital.

I can't forget that. It is my biggest regret.

I asked the nurse to let me know if there was any change. I said I would come straight back. She promised to ring. I had a very bad feeling that night and it was justified. I should never have left.

The hospital rang about eight in the morning and said that Moshe had died. That someone was with him at the time. They hadn't called me. I found out later, that in fact, there was nobody with him. At change over a new nurse had gone into his room and found him dead. I couldn't tell my mother.

But in the car on the way to the hospital I said,

"I think you should prepare for the worst."

She said "No, I am not going to!"

I asked the nurse to tell her because I couldn't.

She said, "Mrs. Berman, your husband died."

My mother said, "What are you talking about? No!"

We went into his room.

DEATH

The room was still. He was lying on his back in bed, wearing his navy blue, striped pyjamas. His dark brown eyes still open; thick black hair combed back and in place. Barely a grey hair in his head.

I sat on the bed next to him. I rubbed his hollow chest.

His body was still warm. I thought I saw his eyes move. They looked alive, still seeing.

My mother stroked his left arm, bent her head down onto it, kissed it and sobbed.

I held onto her as we both walked out of the hospital room, down the long, long corridor and out into the street.

In the car, driving down the main highway from Southport towards Surface Paradise she said,

"He shouldn't have died."

I agreed, "No he shouldn't."

Referring to God, she continued, "He took away my mother and my father and now my husband. It isn't fair. What have I done? What sins have I committed? Is it because I was a Communist? I thought it was right, back then, before the War. I never really believed in it, all that much, but there wasn't anything else. We thought that was the answer, that we could change the world. Am I being punished for that now?"

"Oh, what am I going to do? I don't know anyone in Melbourne. I haven't told anyone I'm coming."

"You're coming to my place," I said.

Raising her right hand in a flamboyant gesture,

"Oh! Thank you, Esther. Thank you, God, for giving me Esther. I'm having a rest now. I'm having a rest from talking" and then changing her tone and for no reason that I could see, she said,

"Oh, don't be so high and mighty."

We drove the rest of the way home in silence.

THE MOVE

When we arrived back at my parents' apartment that morning I began ringing people to let them know what had happened. I rang Home Help, informing them that their services would no longer be required. I also contacted a few people from the local synagogue, some relatives and friends and I was arranging, to bring my father's body back to Melbourne for the funeral.

I spoke to my cousin Michael who wanted to organise things for me, from Melbourne. He said he would contact the Chevra Kedisha, [Jewish funeral directors;] and they would take care of everything, from getting my father's body back, to the service and the burial.

That was an enormous help. I knew my father had a great deal of time for Michael and it was Michael who I asked to speak at his funeral.

Michael's body is buried a few rows away from my parents, in the same cemetery.

MY DAUGHTER

My daughter flew up to Queensland for the day in order to help me and to bring Eva back to Melbourne. I packed some of Eva's clothes and wrote an obituary for the Jewish news while Zoe cleaned the apartment.

I found the drive to the airport particularly difficult. I could not bear to listen to my mother rambling on in the back seat. She was completely disorientated. The death had unhinged her slightly. It was indeed fortunate that my daughter was there to take over when I just couldn't. Gently and patiently talking to her and later on walking with her. Her help was invaluable.

Late that night in my apartment, my mother, in my bed, while I was in the smaller bedroom, I heard her restlessly tossing and turning. She called out "Where's Moshe?"

I went into the room and quietly said, "He died Mum." "Auy," she said despairingly and pitifully.

In Queensland just before my father's death, I had been able to get both of my parents into a Jewish nursing home in Melbourne but then I received a phone call from one of Eva's old friends, who heard that my father had died. She suggested the nursing home where she resided, as an alternative, it happened to be a couple of streets away from my apartment.

Our application was successful. It seemed to be a Godsend and initially, I think it was.

I had just been offered a contract position at a secondary college but would not have been able to accept it had it not been for my pregnant daughter. She already had a toddler. She took my suffering mother, who could not be left by herself at all, into to her home. It would be a week before her room at the nursing home, was to become available.

It was also my daughter, who took my mother to the nursing home for her first visit, where Eva said,

"You're not going to leave me, here are you?"

BALANCING

Zoe Naylor, Toby Krasna

Steffan Krasna, Zoe Naylor

And my hard-working son-in-law, a surfing enthusiast, in his spare time, who also spent time with her and was the one who went to inspect a couple of nursing homes so that we could select the most appropriate one for Eva.

So, for a short time I was able to immerse myself in teaching art and did not allow myself to think about the ongoing tragedy.

When I thought Eva had settled in a little, I told her that I would not be able to visit for a few days. I was returning to Queensland to clean out her apartment and move her belongings back to Melbourne.

I took two unpaid, days, off work and left for Queensland.

RETURNING TO MELBOURNE

I found her in her room. She was lying on the bed.

"Oh Esther, my prayers have been answered," she said when she saw me.

"What do you mean?"

"I was praying that someone would come for me. What am I doing here?"

"I told you that I was going back to Queensland to clean out your apartment."

"Did you? I must have forgotten. I forget so many things. So many important things. I'm very unhappy."

She eased herself up into a sitting position on the right side of the bed, placing both feet down on the floor facing me.

I prepared her lipstick and hairbrush.

"I miss my husband and I miss my life," she said coming towards me.

"I know," I replied quietly, as I took her arm.

THE FUNERAL
To my father

I watched you being carried away in your coffin and I disassociated myself from the event.

It was nothing to do with me. I kept on talking.

I feel it now though. Yes, now I do feel it.

And when you died, only the good about you remained with me, your pure core.

No.

No hard feelings.

You had so much to deal with and managed it well, single handily. Without discussion, until those last two weeks when you lost heart. You were tired and the tumour, got the better of you. You tried gambling your life back together and you knew that could never have worked.

And after your death, I felt your presence so strongly and you spoke to me and said, "*Ich hob faloiren dem veg.*"

"I lost my way."

PACKING UP

The furniture removers were packing all of my parents belongings. I was sorting the books when I felt my father say, "Be careful here". It was his voice, loud and clear. I went into the kitchen to see how the two men were going. A crystal vase had been broken. I decided not to say anything and went back to packing the books.

It transpired that a whole box full of expensive vases and other items never arrived in Melbourne. The voice was right, "Be careful here".

I had finished cleaning the apartment and was at the sink, close to the stove where Moshe often stood, watching me cook, always checking to see if I was cooking the food the way he liked it.

As I washed some vegetables, I had the strangest feeling that there was someone standing behind me. I turned around and heard his voice again.

"You've done a good job," it said. It felt a little strange. But I was glad he approved.

Also, before we left Queensland for Melbourne, the night of my father's death, Zoe cleaned out all the drawers and cupboards.

When I returned to Queensland to clear the place out entirely, I began checking the cupboards and dressers. Inside one of the drawers in their bedroom I found a piece of paper with hand written instructions from my father, putting me in charge of all his accounts, possessions and business. I don't know how Zoe could have missed it. She had definitely gone through every drawer in the bedroom.

RIPPING BOXES

Back in my apartment in Melbourne, I ripped the masking tape off the boxes and began looking through their contents. I was tearing pages to shreds; old Bank statements, paid bills, words, words and more words. Words translated from Yiddish to English, English words and their meanings, looked up in the dictionary, all written out on various scraps of paper. Hundreds of them. Every time my father came across a word he did not understand, it was written down.

I was shredding parts of his life and throwing them into the rubbish bin. I had to be ruthless.

But what I didn't realise as I was frantically throwing out those slips of paper was that I was throwing away some of his memories. Jotted down in Yiddish at different times and thrown into a drawer.

Luckily a few sheets escaped my massive clean-up. I found them at a later time, when I was searching through some books and I was able to translate them from Yiddish into English, with a little help from one of my neighbours.

Herring, herring salted and peppered

Cleaned and soured

Herring with roe

Herring with milk

Herring, herring

Herring offered in every way

Sour cucumbers

Sauerkraut

Beans round and longish, yellow, green, brown and flecked,

Beans, beans

Cold beans, brown and chopped

Cold Semolina: cold and hearty.

Perfect for a Barley soup

And to the side, for the chicken soup

Buckwheat, buckwheat

Buckwheat offered in every way.

Metaphor
Socks; pony socks,
Little socks as strong as iron
The shoes will fall apart
But these here little socks will remain intact

Another
Heated snow and puffed up importance, both eventually turn to water.

Heated snow and puffed up importance both merge into a pool.

If you build an oven of butter, it melts. If you make yourself a crown based on self-importance, it can never last.

A long piece of spaghetti and a tiny square of pasta You don't have to be worthy if it's meant to be.

On another scrap of paper, I came across some interesting information, which I knew nothing about, also written in Yiddish, and I wondered how many other people were aware of the fact that in 1938, William Cooper aged seventy seven, Secretary of the Aboriginal Advancement League, walked many miles barefooted, with other members of the Yorta Yorta tribe, leading a solitary demonstration to the German Consulate, protesting against the horrendous treatment of Jewish people in Germany.

His aim was to deliver a letter, which stated:

"On behalf of the Aboriginal inhabitants of Australia, we wish to have it registered and on record that we protest wholeheartedly at the cruel persecution of the Jewish people by the Nazi government in Germany.

We plead that you would make it known to your government and its military leaders that this cruel persecution of their fellow citizens must be brought to an end."

However, the German Consul – General at the time would not acknowledge the group and it was not until 2012, exactly 74 years later, that the seventy-four-year-old grandson of William Cooper, Alf "Boydie" Turner, and great grandson, Kevin Russell along with 200 others, including Holocaust survivors and members of the Jewish Community, in a re-enactment of the event, presented a duplicate letter.

It was acknowledged by Michael Pearce, the German honorary consul, who said, that the German Embassy supported the re-enactment of the 1938 protest. "It's been an opportunity to right a wrong from the past."

It was quite incredible, that there was only one record, of a solitary group, a group of Aboriginals, who demonstrated against these inhumane crimes. A group who were, themselves marginalised, and who, at the time, did not even have the right to vote in Australia.

In 2002, Israel dedicated a plaque to William Cooper and members of the Aboriginal Community who bravely demonstrated in 1938 and in 2010 trees were planted in their honour.

AFTERNOON AT THE NURSING HOME

I often sat with my mother at meal times, usually at dinner but on this occasion, it was lunch time. The residents were offered a bowl of ice cream, one of their favourite desserts.

Most of them sat at the same table, with the same people every day. It gave them a sense of security.

Four women were seated at a particular table. Next to the front window. They had been together for quite some years.

The caregiver serving lunch, handed a bowl of ice cream to one of the women, Helen. Causing Sarah, sitting directly opposite her, to cry out in alarm.

"Don't give her that!"

Taking no notice, the Caregiver placed the ice cream onto the table and Helen, with great relish, began to devour it.

"Why didn't you ask them to bring you some from the kitchen, instead of taking mine?" continued Sarah.

"It wasn't yours. You've already had some."

"Where is?"

Sarah said, throwing both arms out to the sides, palms up.

"Where is it?"

"You've eaten it. It's already been taken off the table."

Sarah is dejected. "Oh."

When the table had been cleared Helen closed her eyes and began to doze, her head slowly dropping.

The caregiver placed a cup of tea in front of her. She lifted her head, saw the tea and said,

"I didn't order any tea."

"Just leave it there. You might feel like it later."

The woman waited for a couple of minutes, then raising her finger into the air, as one might when in a restaurant, attracting the attention of a waiter. She called

"Can I have a cake with that?"

THE NURSING HOME
Seemed perfect

The nursing home was clean, sunny, bright and a pleasant looking place with attractive courtyards to sit and walk in. There were numerous activities organised for the residents; concerts and bus trips which my mother usually enjoyed. The food was mostly good. It was very close to my place, making it easy for her to walk home with me for meals.

Jewish people from many different countries around the world lived in the home so my mother was able to utilise her language skills. The whole situation should have been ideal.

BALANCING

Initially, when she adjusted to her new living situation and made a few friends, she coped well.

Once, she and other residents were sitting in a group, in the bright lounge-room. The armchairs were placed in a semi-circle while residents were happily engaged in a game of catch the balloon, with a couple of the caregivers.

While throwing the balloons one of the caregivers greeted me with, "Your mother's been waiting for you today."

My mother quick with her response, said cheerfully, "I wait for her every day!"

On another visit she seemed quite happy even though she was sitting alone. It was after lunch. Usually the residents were moved into the lounge-room or taken outside if it was a sunny or warm day. But my mother was still in the dining room.

She was sitting at the end of the long table with palms upturned, smiling. "*Nu, vos ton mir?*" she asked.

"Well, what are we doing?"

I approached her saying, "Who are you talking to?"

She turned, smiled and said, "A very intelligent person."

I laughed.

AROUND THE TABLE
WITH EVA

My family and I were gathered around the dining room table eating dinner, when my mother asked where her husband was. She always noticed his absence when we were all together as a family.

I said, "He died one year and one month ago."

My children darted a look across the table at her. Her pain seeped into them.

I realised then, that telling her the truth no longer served any purpose at all. I had to alter my approach. Lying would not help but changing the subject would.

If I was quick enough and said something which ignited her interest, I could spare her some intense and overwhelming pain.

There was no point keeping her in the present at all times, particularly in relation to Moshe, her husband of sixty-five years, whom she missed so much and who, since retirement, some fifteen years earlier had been her constant companion.

WHERE'S MOSHE

In the foyer of the nursing home where we sat drinking our hot tea, my mother said casually,

"Oh, my mother's been so strange to me lately. She seems so distant. I don't know why."

"What do you mean your mother? Do you mean your daughter?"

"No, I mean my mother," she said.

"And where's Moshe? Is he really so busy? He just doesn't care about me anymore. Not one thing left." "*Ich ze eim nisht ingantsen.*

"*Er hot genumen ale zeyne zakhn fun shunk aun iz avekgegangen.*

"Nisht kein ein zuch geblibn."

"I don't see Moshe anywhere. He took all of his things out of the cupboard and he left. Not one thing left."

"He doesn't care about me at all."

"He does care about you. Very much," I said.

"Well where is he then?" she asks despairingly.

A change of subject is necessary here, I thought. I think we need to say hello to someone, and quickly.

I noticed one of her caregivers up ahead.

"Hi," I called out.

"Hello. And how are you Eva?" she asked, smiling as she got closer to us.

"Very well thank you."

Eva's deeply entrenched manners kicked in and her mood began to change.

We walked around the nursing home, through the courtyards and passages. In situations, such as these, when her mood has not been good, I recited the story about Nickie,

Nicholas Jack it's your birthday today…

Luckily, my mother also adored my son and loved the story as much as I did, so she listened intently. That immediately cheered her up. But I had no need of any story this time because we could hear children's animated voices up ahead. I simply said,

"Do you hear those voices?"

"Yes."

"Those are the voices of your two great grandchildren." "Oh," she said.

She was besotted with my daughter's children and as we approached them, her joy became more and more evident.

My daughter and her two boys, the oldest then five, shiny brown curls, auburn hues in the light and the younger one, three, with a thick straight blonde fringe cut sharply above his eyebrows, were sitting on the floor, coloured pencils scattered all around them, in the small but bright sitting area at the end of a rather dim passage.

Drawing in their sketchbooks.

When they saw us, they jumped up quickly, yelling,

"Hello Bubba! Hello Bubba!"

My mother and I sat down in the patterned armchairs next to the large glass double doors, which overlooked the church grounds next door.

The oldest boy, returned to his drawing. The three-year-old remained standing in front of Eva. Examining her face. Fascinated by her age.

She affectionately stroked his cheek. "*Du bist a sheyn engegle,*" she said.

"You are a beautiful little boy."

He smiled at her, engaged, knowing by her tone that her words expressed something pleasant.

She was encouraged by his response and repeated, "*Du bist a sheyn engegle.*"

My daughter said, "He won't understand."

But he cheekily repeated, "*Sheyn Engele.*"

"See," my mother said, "I knew he'd catch on."

At the conclusion of my daughters visit, my mother and I resumed our leisurely walk through the passages.

I talked about anything and everything I could think of. She held onto the railing with her left hand and her walker, with the right.

I pushed her walker with my right hand and held on to her arm with my left. She asked me a few questions about my children and we chatted.

At some point I must have let go of her arm.

We approached the café at the end of the passage and turned into the main foyer. I was still talking but not looking in her direction.

Samuel and Toby Krasna

I heard "Where's Mummy?" from one of the private caregivers sitting on the couch with her client. I turned to my left. Where was she? I looked back. And there she was, quite a few paces behind me, still holding onto the rail.

We all laughed. "Come on little mother," I said collecting her. She giggled at my term of endearment and we continued dawdling, through the corridors.

It was five o'clock and dinner time when we returned to her area. She peered into the lounge/dining room, through the double, glass doors and said,

"Oh no, not this again. I can't go back in there."

"Come on, you can have some dinner."

I manoeuvred her and the walker into the lounge section and sat her down on one of the comfortable high back chairs.

"Oh, don't go yet, stay a little longer."

Obligingly I said, "Ok, just for a little while then."

I brought a tray over from the food trolley and encouraged her to eat. Luckily it was something she liked, latkes.

She said, "What's going to happen? Am I just going to die here?"

My heart ached and I wished it could have been different.

"I don't know, I'm sure things will improve."

But I thought, that probably will be the outcome. She trusted me implicitly and so her anxiety was alleviated, for that moment anyway.

I made her a cup of tea and we said goodbye until tomorrow.

RETURNING THAT NIGHT

I went home and had a quick meal then decided to go back just to see if my mother was alright. She seemed so defeated when I left. It was only seven o'clock and they had already put her into bed.

I took a cup of tea to her room. The door was shut and it was dark. It looked like they had given her a sedative because she said half dazed,

"Esther, why did you come back?"

"I thought I'd come back and have a cup of tea with you."

She said, "You wouldn't have come if you didn't think there was something wrong. Is it alright?"

"Yes, it's alright."
"Are you sure?"
"Yes, I'm sure."
"It's alright now?" she repeated.
"Yes, of course it's alright."
"Well, if you're sure it's alright, goodnight."

Amused, I picked up my empty cup and left. The next day she was fine.

I SAID THEY COULD RING

Many a night the phone rang. It was at about nine o'clock at night, when a nurse phoned me. I was familiar with these calls and certainly did not look forward to them. She told me that my mother was behaving badly. That she had thrown her teeth across the room after dinner.

"Now she's standing at the door screaming, Ma, Ma! Ma, Ma! She says she wants to go home. I can't get her to go to bed. Will you speak to her?" "Yes, if she wants to speak to me." My mother came to the phone.

"Hi Mum."

"Esther?"

"Yes. How are you?"

I tried to make light conversation and she quietened down.

"The nurse told me that they want you to go to bed."

"Do they now?"

"Are you going to?"

"I don't know, I'll see."

That was never a good sign.

"And Mum, stop calling your mother." A primal reaction, I know.

"I won't."

"But it doesn't do you any good."

"I don't care!"

"Your mother isn't alive anymore."

"Oh, don't be silly Esther!"

And on that note, we said goodnight.

As soon as she put the phone down she wanted to go home again and so they gave her a sedative.

THE FOLLOWING DAY

The following day she was overly subdued and said that she could not walk. She was massively bruised and did not seem to remember what had happened to her.

I reminded her of our conversation and told her what the nurses had said. She made a tremendous effort to concentrate and certain events from the preceding night began to reconnect with her. She told me that she had a bad feeling about a certain staff member and was aware that something untoward had happened, but that she did not know what it was.

TOWARDS THE END
OF HER LIFE

Towards the end of her life, when her memory was fading and words eluded her, with various episodes at the nursing home such as, throwing her teeth across the room and sometimes forgetting how to use her cutlery, times when she yelled, "They're taking the children! They're taking the children!" be assured, that she could still be quite lucid and she still had the ability to censor her words when they were about to become less than tactful.

When she was in hospital with her shattered hip and deep skin lesion, at one point she was crying out "Auy,

Auy, Auy, Auy, Auy," in tremendous pain. I sat on the bed next to her and said, commiserating, I thought,

"Are you in a lot of pain Mum?"

She suddenly stopped mid Auy, looked me straight in the eye and said, "No!" We both laughed and she went back to her crying.

ANOTHER CALL

"Your mother has some skin tears. We don't know how she got them. She has very fine skin and it breaks easily."

The next day, I noticed that her cuts were covered with bandages. The nurses had decided that she was to wear tubi bands to protect her from any further damage. Tubi bands are bandages, which completely cover the legs or arms.

I tried to have them change their decision as the bands restricted her movement considerably. Sometime during the week, she complained that she was unable to walk and to her relief, I removed them. However, it was evident that the bandages were covering severe bruising.

I requested her doctor's opinion. He said that ultimately, it would be my decision, if she were to wear the tubi bands, or not. But the nurses persisted and reluctantly I gave in to their demands.

When I asked the nurses why she was always so bruised, their response was, "Nobody is hurting your mother." "What a strange thing to say. Then why is my mother so bruised? Look at the sore, above her eye? It was never that size. You should have let me know, she'll have to see a specialist about that. It could be Cancer. There are marks on her face, eyes. Her hands…arms… and the huge gash on her leg. Injection marks on her arms.

The residents and their families were also shaken by Eva's appearance.

I had to call the Aged Care Complaints Commission twice. As a consequence of their first visit, the recommendations and procedures at the nursing home, home for the aged, were reviewed and altered.

It would have been so simple to see who was going into my mother's room at night. They would have known anyway. Cameras are installed throughout the building and also in the car park.

At one time, my mother had a huge, painful and very infected gash on her leg. Eventually, when I realised that it was not going to heal, I took her to a specialist. His opinion was that a gash like that would have been caused by a massive knock into stairs or something very sharp. With his help, it was gone in a matter of weeks. But the nursing home continued to say that they had no idea where it came from.

There was a lump on her eyelid, which was covered over by a Band-Aid. When I removed the Band-Aid, I noticed the sore had grown to an enormous size. I immediately took her to a specialist who said it was cancer. We went to the Alfred hospital for radiation treatment every day for two weeks. The treatment was successful.

WOUNDED

It was after eleven that night when the telephone rang. It was Maria, a nurse, from the nursing home. She informed me that Eva had hurt her leg and that she also had a skin tear. I thought it was just another one of the many phone calls I received at night and questioned the degree of damage. I said I would see her in the morning.

Maria insisted that I come straight away. I then heard someone crying in the background. I had a very bad feeling and got dressed immediately.

I rang the front door bell of the nursing home but there was no answer. They were expecting me. Where were they? I stood outside ringing for five minutes then used my mobile to contact them. Finally, a nurse came to the front door and let me in.

As we walked down the passage towards my mother's room I could hear loud screams.

"What happened?" I asked my mother as I entered the room.

She showed her "skin tear" which was a deep cut on her leg. There was fresh blood on her body and night gown.

She spoke quickly, in Yiddish. "*Zie hot mir tzu Shnayden! Zie hot mir tsu shayden!*" "She cut me! She cut me!

"*Zi hot mir aza a klap gegebn!*" Indicating her hip, she told me who had been in her room. "She gave me such a knock." "*Wer?*" I asked. "Who?" "*Zie.*" She said, "Her."

"*Vos shteyt du?*" "Who stands here?"

"*Yo.*" "Yes."

The nurse did not look at all comfortable and asked me what she was saying.

My mother described it verbally, in Yiddish and physically, her hands playing out the trauma; her fingers dancing around, perfectly describing the situation, her language clear and fluent. Suddenly, exquisitely lucid, it poured out of her. It was as though the events of the night had somehow brought her back to her senses.

A woman desperate to relay the hideous abuse perpetrated upon her in the hour prior to my arrival.

The nurse stood at the end of the bed repeating, "What is she saying. What is she saying?" "What does this mean *tsu shayden?*"

Although shocked, I ignored the nurse and calmly kept listening to my mother's emotional outpouring.

She left the room and came back with the nurse in charge who began asking me the same question in her thick Russian accent.

"What does this mean '*tsu shayden*'?"

I continued the conversation with my mother and once again, did not reply. Eventually the two nurses left the room and I waited for the ambulance.

In the early hours of the morning, two ambulance officers arrived. They had been ringing and waiting at the front door, as I had, to be admitted by a staff member. But no one from the facility had responded. Finally, they let themselves in with their special swipe card.

The ambulance officers then spoke to the nurse in charge, asking her for some details about my mother's injuries. However, she was not forthcoming, speaking quietly and looking down at the floor.

They were appalled and told me that they thought the entire situation was dealt with in a very unprofessional manner.

I had not confronted the nurses about what had taken place that night, as I intended to seek legal advice.

In fact, a couple of days later, after writing a letter stating that I would be removing my mother from the nursing home, my daughter and I went to pick up her things. A nurse asked me if Eva remembered anything about what happened to her.

In retrospect I wish I had confronted those present, that night, then and there because my mother died before any action could be taken and they did not have to answer for any of their abuse.

But then again if you believe, as I do, that ultimately, we all have to answer for all of our actions in life, their actions will indeed be accounted for. Why doesn't that make me feel any better?

HOSPITAL

At the hospital, after my mother's injuries had been checked, I was informed that her hip had been utterly shattered. The doctor was not sure that she would ever walk again and if it did improve enough, she would need months of painful physiotherapy. He said, it was not the usual fracture associated with old people. He also acknowledged the large gash on her leg.

My mother was quite amazing. Yes, she had been screaming in pain. She was ninety-two years old. Imagine how intense the pain would be with someone crushing your hip with a hammer and cutting into your flesh?

An assault like that on any person is a low and cruel act to say the least but to do that to a ninety-two-year-old woman? What sort of person does that? It can only be described as brutal and criminal.

Did they think her life was worthless or somehow less important than theirs? Maybe, because she was not a socialite, neither were her children doctors or judges. Did they think that she was so demented that they could use her as they pleased? That she would not remember anything?

A nurse gave my mother an injection of pethidine or something similar for the pain and Eva relaxed a little.

She said they would take her up into a ward and advised me to go home. It was already morning.

Some hours later when I rang to inquire about her condition I was informed that her screams had disturbed the rest of the ward and that an ambulance would be taking her to the Caulfield hospital.

I visited a lawyer and in detail feverishly blurted out the horrific events, which led to my being in his office. He listened carefully, taking notes as I spoke, intermittently reacting and giving his opinion, voicing clearly and forcefully, that one should be able to leave a loved one safely in a nursing home. He agreed to take on the case, free of charge. That in itself said a great deal.

It was the first time I had related the entire story to anyone, bits and pieces to this person and that, but never the whole story.

CAULFIELD HOSPITAL VISITING HOURS

A week or so after my mother had been admitted the doctor asked me what I thought about her ongoing care.

"Do you really want to prolong her life?" he said. "Let her go."

"No, I can't do that. It's not up to me."

"Don't you think she's suffering enough?"

"Yes, I can see she's suffering."

I took a breath and turned to my mother,

"Do you want to die Mum?"

The response? An unequivocal "No."

THE MAN BESIDE ME

It was after visiting hours but it was necessary for me to take a few things over to the hospital so, when I arrived it was relatively quiet. The lights in the wards were all out and most of the patients, including my mother, were asleep.

I sat at the end of her bed. It had been lowered onto the floor to eliminate any danger of falling.

After a while she opened her eyes and said quietly, "If you do bad..." then she stopped.

"Yes, if you do bad.... What have you ever done that's bad?"

'I know bad things are happening to us, aren't they?"

"Yes," I said.

"But I don't know why," she continues.

I waited.

"Be careful Esther."

She was quiet again, then,

"I know they're hurting you." I didn't say anything.

"How are you really?"

"Good."

"Are you sure?"

"I'm, here aren't I?"

Exhausted she closed her eyes.

I hear my father, "I can't help you Esther. I can't help you."

She continues,

"I'm waiting for something good to happen in our lives Esther."

"Me too, Mum."

We're still holding hands.

She looked to the side of where I was sitting.

"The man with you."

'Where?" I turned around.

"The one with you." "Is he nice?" I ask.

She was definitely staring at something and listening very carefully.

"He says he's nice. He is going somewhere with you."

"What does he look like?"

She waited and concentrated. "I don't know." Then, "He's gone."

I believed her because it has been documented that people close to death see and hear dead relatives, for example, Visions, Trips and Crowded Rooms, by David Kessler, who worked closely with people nearing death. And she had made similar comments to me before. For instance, "The little children are here," or a certain relative was there, or, "I don't like the look of that one." Also, sometimes she appeared to be holding someone's hand.

MY MOTHER'S DEATH
January 21 2013

I had been asking for a doctor to come and examine my mother Eva, for two weeks. I said, "Listen to her chest. She's wheezing so badly." I had probably approached every nurse on duty. I even asked one of the nurses if the chesty noise she was making was the death rattle.

"No," she said, "she's got a long way to go yet."

Sometimes the nurses came in equipped to take her blood pressure and temperature. Everything according to them was quite normal.

A doctor was called and I asked him to prescribe some antibiotics for her throat. She had been complaining of soreness and an inability to swallow. Not just to me. She had told a family friend, who visited every week and who also fed her lunch on those occasions, that she was unable to eat as she felt that there was an obstruction in her throat. The doctor said that he would write a script but he did not.

I could see that my mother was distressed and in pain.

On Thursday, the day before her death I asked a number of nurses to call a doctor. Finally, I went to her caseworker and vehemently insisted. She told me that my mother had been fine in the morning. I persisted. A physiotherapist arrived with a stethoscope. She listened to my mother's breathing, placing the stethoscope in different positions on her back.

"She sounds fine to me," she said.

"Listen to her chest," I said.

She humoured me and did as I asked.

"Oh," she said, "I think she does need a doctor."

The doctor was called and before I left that evening, I asked if he would ring me after he had examined my mother. Of course, I did not realise how bad she really was because during my visit that day, she had gripped my hands with so much strength, it surprised me.

The doctor was a locum and he did ring. It was about eleven o'clock at night. He said that my mother was suffocating. An ambulance was called.

I arrived as she was being wheeled out of the nursing home. I could hear OH, OH, OH, OH, OH, loudly as I drove up. She had an oxygen mask covering her face. I went over to her,

"Mum!"

One of the ambulance officers said that she was critical and could not respond to me and that they were going to take her to the Alfred Hospital. I should take my car, he said, as they would be working on her on the way.

I rang my son and arranged to meet him there.

My mother was already in emergency when we got there. She was lying on a bed hooked up to some equipment. She was still moaning but not quite as badly as before. They had given her some morphine for the pain and told me that she had a collapsed lung and pneumonia and may not survive. What did I want them to do? I said everything possible to help her.

The doctor came back with a pen and paper and proceeded to question me as to what extent he should go to in order to help Eva. Did I want him to restart her heart if it failed?

"No," I said. "If that happened, her life would have taken its course. But I want you to do everything possible to make her comfortable and help her as much as you can."

They gave her antibiotics and a little more morphine. She seemed to improve. Even the nurse said she appeared better and that they might take her up to a ward for the night.

I talked to her, stroked her brow and kissed her. My son, Nick and I held her hands.

Nick said that according to the monitor, she seemed to improve with the sound of my voice.

I said, "Mum."

She opened her eyes.

"It's me, Esther."

She looked directly at me with her pale blue watery eyes.

"Look, Nickie's here."

My son put his face close to hers, so that she could see him.

"Eva."

She strained her eyes, focusing on him for a moment. I'm sure she saw him but then her eyes closed again.

While Nick and I were talking I noticed that my mother was crying. We don't really cry much in our family.

The nurse handed me a tissue and I wiped the corners of her eyes.

"She doesn't want to leave," I said to the doctor who had just come in again.

He looked over at her and replied,

"She's a very strong lady."

The first doctor left for the night and another one replaced him; a young woman. She came in to speak to us and said that things did not look good. She wanted to turn the monitor off. Maybe she thought that it was giving us false hope.

The machine was switched off and the room was eerily still, except for my mother's rhythmic gasping.

One of the nurses came in and asked me if I wanted my mother cleaned up. I thought it was a good idea at the time but in retrospect, I would have said no don't bother, thank you.

She left the room and came back with another nurse and Nick and I went into the waiting room.

We were called back into the cubicle as my mother was literally taking her last couple of breaths. The nurse had come to collect us and said that Eva was worse than she thought and we should hurry.

We sat down next to her. She was on her side. They had taken the oxygen mask off her face and replaced it with fine breathing tubes. I do not even know if it was switched on. It was so very quiet. My mother was not making a sound. We sat down close to her. She took one little breath, barely audible, followed by another, her last.

"Oh Mum."

I was the one sobbing now, my son comforting me.

I stood at the door looking back at her body. In fifteen short minutes my beautiful mother had become a corpse, her curved fingers stiffening. Her unusually fine skin and warm complexion now pearl white. Without a trace of tension on her formerly lined brow; smooth, smooth white, white skin.

It struck me that her hair, her light brown hair with the grey roots that needed doing, seemed so long. She had both arms outstretched to one side, her mouth slightly open. She did not want to die but it seemed that when the last breath left her body, her spirit had no desire to linger.

I thought of my father for whom I had not been able to grieve properly. Even a few hours after his death, when we walked into the hospital room, he still looked like one of the living.

And later, as I have said, I felt his presence a number of times.

I had asked him why he didn't go.

He said, "I'm waiting for Mum." And earlier that afternoon, she had been calling his name.

THE BURIAL

She was buried on Friday afternoon, the same day she died. I wanted it that way because I thought that if I did not organise it then, I might not have been able to organise it at all. So, there was no time to invite anyone else to attend and close family from interstate, understandably, needed more notice than they were given.

The only ones in attendance were, the Rabbi, another man, my son, my daughter and me. I could not take in her death at the time, I just went through the motions but my children valued the experience.

The coffin arrived and as with my father I pushed all grieving aside. I distanced myself from the event.

The prayers were read. I tore my clothes. We walked to the gravesite; the casket was lowered into the ground and we all had turn of shovelling dirt onto the coffin until the plot was filled. More prayers and then we said goodbye to the Rabbi and the other man.

FINALITY

The consecration for both of my parents was later, in October, the same month as my mother's birthday. It was there that I really said good-bye to my parents. That was the funeral for me. I felt the full impact of their death on that day.

There, I was able to say a few words about each of them, to family and friends who had come to commemorate with us, stopping only for a moment, to overcome my emotion, when it came to speaking about my mother.

It was there that I said, "You can't hold on to the dead." But some time later, I realised that I had, for far longer than I should have.

At the cemetery my mother and father lay side by side in a double monument; I imagined them holding hands the way they had done in life.

Prior to the consecration, I had nightmares about them almost every night but after the consecration, the nightmares seemed to subside.

It was as if the prayers and the words spoken at the consecration had made them more settled somehow, and then in turn, so was I.

LOOKING IN

I am in my parents' kitchen looking into their lives. I'm standing in front of the curtains, which cover large floor to ceiling windows. The kitchen table, where my mother is sitting is in front of me. But I can't be seen. I'm a ghost in the room.

My mother is dressed in a flattering mauve purple coloured, long sleeved shirt, a pair of semi-stretch fawn slacks and light tan court shoes. Her serene face tanned, lined, revealing too many moments exposed to the sun's damaging rays.

My father's hair was loose, mussed, as though he had just woken from one of his afternoon naps. Bone knee length shorts with angled side pockets, in which he stuffed his many keys and one large brown and white striped, clean handkerchief for the day. He wore a pair of off-white walking shoes; his thin legs still well-muscled. A light brown patterned open neck short-sleeved shirt, covering tanned, once muscular arms.

He is at the bench quietly singing in his low, low voice and making two cups of tea. It's more like a chant really, a chant, reminiscent of Hasidic singing.

He brings a cup over to my mother. She looks up, and thanks him and he goes back to the bench to collect his own cup.

He puts it on the table and sits down in his usual position directly opposite her.

I'm standing behind him wedged in between the curtain and the chair next to his. There are no words spoken, just the chanting.

They sip their tea.

"Life should have been more balanced, shouldn't it, Dad?" I said in the stillness.

He has both hands around his cup.

The singing stops. He looks straight ahead.

"*Yo*," he says quietly in his deep voice.

My mother looks up, not in my direction, just upwards.

"*Oy, Esther croyn*," she says lovingly.

"Oh, Esther darling."

Balancing

I really miss my parents and I think about them a lot; their lives, their triumphs, their relationship; the way they interacted with one another and how it so often made me laugh. And how every Sunday morning at eleven o'clock they sat quietly facing each other at the wrought iron legged, kitchen table, perfectly cleaned after a just eaten breakfast, radio placed on the right-hand side, listening closely to the Jewish hour. The way they still held hands when they went for a walk, or sat on the couch watching television, or even lying on the bed for a nap. I think about their struggles and ultimately their suffering and that always breaks my heart.

Eva and Moshe Berman

LIST OF DECEASED FAMILY MEMBERS

DANCYGIER
Sholem DANZIGIER
Born Lodz Poland
Approximate age 57
Murdered in Chelmno concentration camp

Wife
Perl DANZIGIER
Born in Constantine
Approximate age 55
Murdered in Chelmno death camp

Children
Shlomo DANZIGIER
Approximate age 30
A merchant. Engaged in Rabbinical studies.
Assumed murdered.

Fraidl GOLDBERG [nee DANZIGIER]
Born in Lodz, in 1908 Assumed murdered

Braine DANZIGIER
Born in Lodz Poland
Approximate age 25
Murdered in Chelmno death camp

Harshl DANZIGIER
Born in Lodz Poland
Approximate age 25-28
Employed in a shop
Murdered in Chelmno death camp

Hena DANZIGIER
Born in 1925
Wloclawek Poland
Approximate age 17
Murdered in Chelmno death camp

Toba DANZIGIER
Born in Wloclawek in 1928
Approximate age 16
Murdered in Chelmno death camp.

KOWADLO

Great grandparents

Eliezer Meir KOWADLO
A Cantor and Mohel was born 1871 in Ostrolenka, Ostroleka zgierski, Bialystok Voivodeship, Poland. He was the first child of Zorach KOWADLO and Bejla GUTMAN

Wife

Michla KOWADLO: Michla, TANDETNIK was born in 1871. She was the first child of Froim TANDETNIK and Fejga PERETZMAN.

Children

Izak Efroim KOWADLO

Born in the late 1883, one of nine children.
Place of Residence Wloclawek Poland
Murdered in Chelmno death camp in 1942

Wife

Esther KOWADLO [nee KOWALSKI]

Born in 1894
Lived in Wloclawek
Murdered in Chelmno death camp

Children
Ruth KOWADLO
Born in 1924
Wloclawek Poland
Murdered in Chelmno death camp

Zygmus KOWADLO
Born in 1928
Wloclawek Poland
Murdered in Chelmno death camp
"May their souls be bound up in the bond of eternal life."

GLOSSARY

Afakoiman	A piece of Matzos used for a game. It is hidden from the children. They search during the Seder.
Chametz	Any food containing flour or yeast.
Charoses	A mixture of grated apples, nuts, fruit, cinnamon and spices mixed with red wine. Resembling mortar and bricks made by the Jews when they were slaves in Egypt.
Chazeres	A bitter herb, usually Romaine lettuce and grated horseradish symbolising the bitterness Jews experienced when they were slaves in Egypt.

Haggadah	A book of songs and texts which establish the order of proceedings at the Passover Seder.
Karpas	Vegetables, such as celery, parsley and boiled potatoes. It is dipped into salted water.
Maror	Bitter herbs, such as Romaine lettuce and horseradish.
Matzos	Bread baked without yeast.
Seder	A family gathering to celebrate God freeing the Jewish people from slavery, in Egypt.

www.ingramcontent.com/pod-product-compliance
Lightning Source LLC
Chambersburg PA
CBHW042131160426
43199CB00021B/2877